Sew Your Stress Away

A Guide to Inner Peace

by

Maxine Campbell

Table of Contents

Maxine's Empowering Journey From Midwife to Sewing Tutor 1

Stitch 1: Sewing for Mental Health 9

Stitch 2: Getting Started with Sewing 22

Stitch 3: The Art of Breathing and Relaxation 62

Stitch 4: Nurturing Your Well-being 69

Stitch 5: Empowerment Through Creativity 79

Stitch 6: Rediscovering Joy in the Modern World 92

Stitch 7: Teaching Students to Love Themselves 107

Stitch 8: A Workbook for Sewing and Well-being 118

Conclusion 152

Maxine's Empowering Journey From Midwife to Sewing Tutor

Let's begin our journey into the world of sewing, creativity, and well-being. My background in Nursing and Midwifery has given me a unique perspective on the importance of self-care and mental health. But it was my love for sewing that truly opened my eyes to the transformative power of creativity as a means to relax, unwind, and find inner peace.

In this book, we'll explore the profound connection between sewing and mental well-being, and I'll guide you through the art of using needle and thread to not only create beautiful projects but also to nurture your soul.

Over the years, I've witnessed firsthand the positive impact that sewing can have on individuals of all ages, from young children to those in their golden years. This book is a culmination of my experiences, research, and the stories of countless students who have discovered the joy of sewing as a path to happiness and fulfillment.

The Power of Sewing for Relaxation and Well-being

In today's fast-paced world, where the constant demands of the ever-changing landscape can leave us feeling perpetually frazzled, the pursuit of tranquility becomes a precious endeavor. My personal journey into the world of sewing was motivated by a profound yearning for peace amidst the whirlwinds of a busy life. Having spent years as a midwife in a bustling delivery suite, where the ebb and flow of life's beginnings and endings were daily occurrences, I stumbled upon an unexpected haven – the art of sewing.

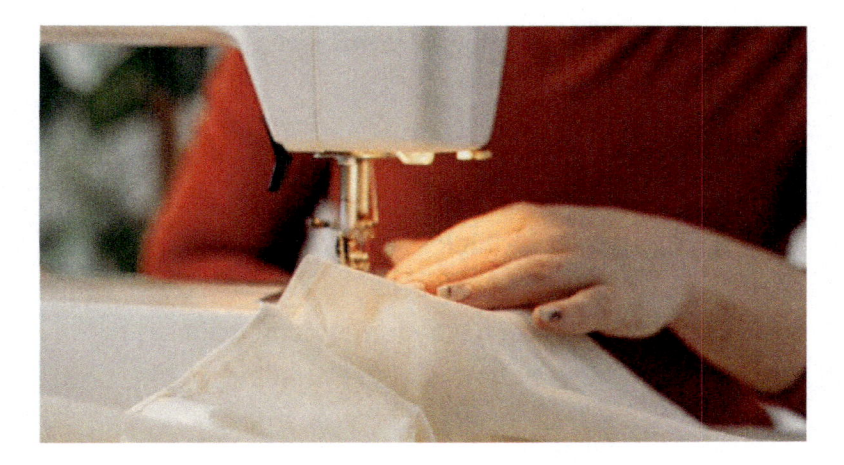

Sewing, I soon realized, is more than a craft; it's a gateway to self-discovery, an avenue to emotional equilibrium, and a means to nurture one's soul. It quickly became my sanctuary, a place where I could momentarily detach from the clamor of the outside world, gather my thoughts, and embark on a journey of creation using my own hands. During these peaceful moments, I discovered the remarkable capacity of sewing to soothe racing thoughts, alleviate stress, and evoke a sense of serenity. The rhythmic flow of the needle through the fabric, the tactile connection with textiles, and the tangible act of crafting something beautiful held a therapeutic enchantment.

However, my exploration of the therapeutic realm of sewing extended beyond personal solace; it unearthed the profound benefits it offers to mental well-being. Sewing is not merely a pastime; it is a gentle yet potent practice that provides a gentle escape from daily life and, at the same time, facilitates a reconnection with oneself. It is a nurturing force for emotional health and a conduit to finding inner peace.

By delving deeper into the art of sewing and its profound impact on relaxation and well-being, this book aims to shed light on how this timeless craft can transform lives. It invites you to embark on a journey of self-discovery, creativity, and inner calm – a journey that promises to unlock the soothing potential of every stitch.

How It All Began

It all began on the momentous day when I bid farewell to my midwifery career. After dedicating more than three decades of my professional life to the NHS, I made the decision to 'live my best life' in 2018. Early retirement meant years of adventure and exploration awaited me as soon as I took off my scrubs.

Unintentionally, I found myself returning to old hobbies and routines. This period of relaxation sparked the rekindling of my passion for sewing and dressmaking. Since then, sewing has brought me immense pleasure, providing a space for me to unwind as time slips away. I've devoted numerous hours each day to mastering standard techniques and experimenting with new ones.

When the pandemic swept the world, like thousands of others, I spent my days sewing and tuning into the Sewing Bee on television. There was a revived interest in the traditional skill of sewing, with millions of people now annually tuning in to the extremely popular Sewing Bee program.

I initially launched an online sewing class with some of my nursing and midwifery colleagues to offer support and foster a sense of community during the pandemic. It blossomed into a wonderful sewing community. This marked the beginning of my journey in teaching people how to sew and the establishment of my business, Artisan Sewing School.

Opening a sewing school in Milnsbridge is my way of giving back to the community. Currently, I am a Registered Midwife (RM), Nurse (RGN), and Childbirth Coach. Holding qualifications including City and Guild Fashion Level 2, a Level 3 in pattern cutting, and a PGCE (Postgraduate Certificate in Education), I am also a qualified mental health first aider, a cause I am deeply passionate about.

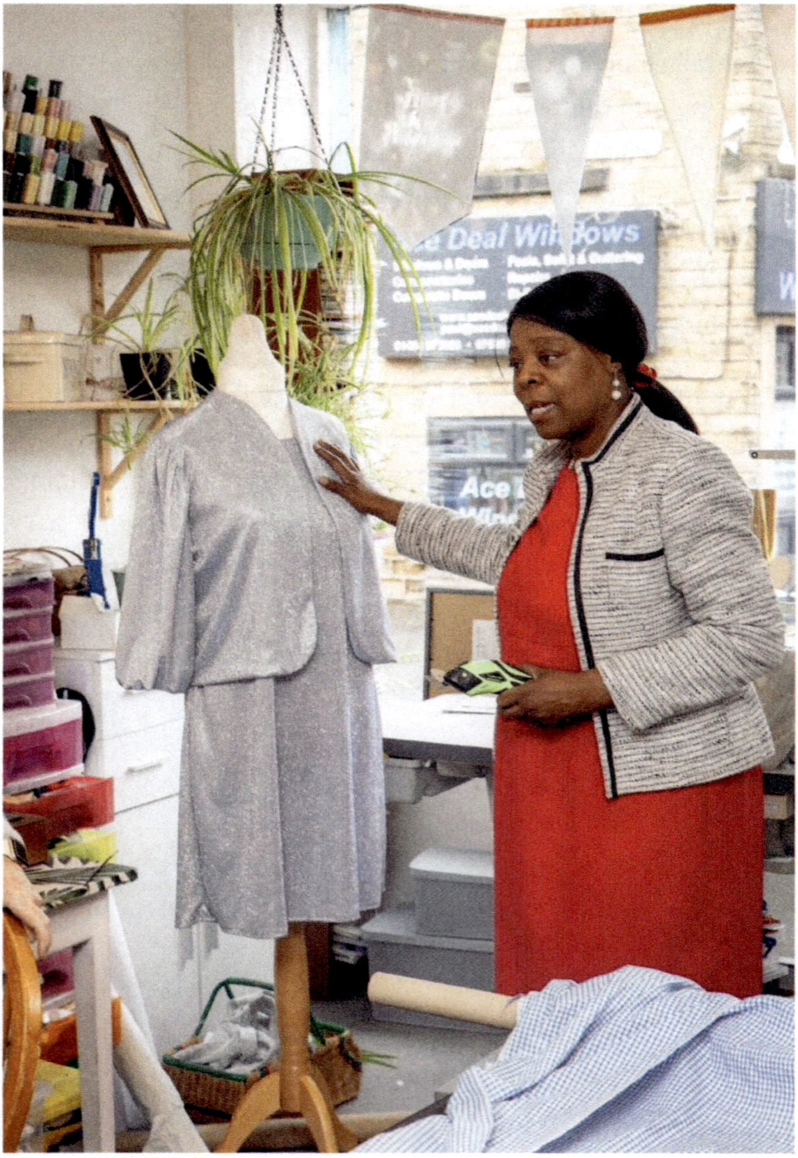

Why This Book Matters

In a world often characterized by the ever-increasing demands of modern life, it's easy to lose sight of the essential elements that contribute to our overall well-being. We find ourselves perpetually connected to screens, inundated with notifications, and caught in the ceaseless race of the digital age. Amid this noise and discord, the significance of self-care, mindfulness, and nurturing our mental health can sometimes fade into the background.

This book is more than just a compilation of sewing techniques; it's a heartfelt demonstration of the amazing impact the art of sewing can have on our lives, transcending the mere act of crafting with needle and thread. It is a call to rekindle our connection with a simple yet deeply therapeutic, practice. It is an invitation to rediscover the joy of slowing down, of feeling the textures of fabric under our fingertips, and of witnessing the transformation of raw materials into beautiful creations.

In these pages, we embark on a journey that extends far beyond the realm of sewing itself. We explore how engaging in creative endeavors can act as a beacon of light in our lives, a refuge from the storm, and a means to restore the balance between the digital world and our inner selves. We delve into the science behind the therapeutic effects of sewing, unearthing the biological mechanisms that release dopamine, serotonin, and oxytocin, contributing to a profound sense of happiness and fulfillment.

This book also holds the promise of empowerment. It reminds us that regardless of age or skill level, we possess within us the capacity to believe in ourselves, nurture our self-esteem, and take pride in our achievements, no matter how seemingly small. It is the idea that creative pursuits, like sewing, have the power to empower individuals, build their self-confidence, and instill a deep sense of self-worth.

Moreover, this book carries a message of community and refocusing our priorities in the modern age. It speaks to the importance of fostering a sense of togetherness and shared purpose, especially during times of isolation and detachment.

In essence, this book matters because it shines a light on the timeless practice of sewing and how it can be a powerful catalyst for personal transformation, mental well-being, and community building. It is a reminder that, In the midst of our fast-paced, technology-driven lives, there exists a world of creativity, self-discovery, and genuine connection waiting to be explored – one stitch at a time.

Stitch 1: Sewing for Mental Health

In the modern era, as our lives become increasingly hectic and interconnected, the importance of mental health and well-being cannot be overstated. The stresses and demands of everyday existence can often leave us feeling frazzled, anxious, and overwhelmed. It's in this tumultuous landscape that we embark on a journey, guided by the gentle and therapeutic art of sewing, toward a state of enhanced mental clarity, emotional balance, and inner serenity.

In this chapter, we'll explore the unique connection between sewing and mental health and the ways in which the simple act of sewing can act as a balm for the mind and the soul. It's a journey into the realm of creative expression, mindfulness, and self-care, all of which play pivotal roles in nurturing our mental well-being.

As a midwife with years of experience working in a busy delivery suite, I have witnessed firsthand the emotional rollercoaster of life's beginnings and farewells. In this high-stress environment, sewing became my personal refuge, where I could momentarily escape the chaos and reconnect with my inner self.

In the pages that follow, we will delve into the research and science that underpin the benefits of sewing for mental health. We'll uncover the neurobiological processes at play, including the release of dopamine, serotonin, and oxytocin, which contribute to a sense of happiness and contentment during sewing sessions.

Whether you're seeking a respite from the daily grind or an avenue for self-expression, sewing has the potential to become a therapeutic anchor in your life.

Sewing as a Therapeutic Activity

Sewing, once considered a traditional craft, has emerged as an unexpected hero in this pursuit of calm and tranquility. At its core, sewing is a rhythmic and repetitive activity. The gentle back-and-forth motion of the needle, the careful selection of fabrics, and the measured pace of each stitch create a harmonious rhythm. This rhythm has a unique ability to draw us into the present moment, inviting a state of mindfulness that is often elusive in our fast-paced lives.

When you sew, you enter a world where time slows down, and the worries of yesterday and tomorrow fade into the background. Your focus narrows to the task at hand - the careful alignment of seams, the choice of thread color, and the steady progression of your project. This singular focus serves as a form of meditation, allowing you to temporarily detach from the anxieties and stressors that may plague your mind.

In this therapeutic process, the act of sewing engages not only your hands but also your heart and mind. It's a holistic experience that encourages you to engage your senses fully. You feel the textures of fabric beneath your fingertips, hear the gentle rustling of materials, and see your creations take shape before your eyes. This multisensory engagement promotes a sense of connection to the present moment, a fundamental aspect of mindfulness.

Moreover, sewing is an activity that offers tangible results. As you progress with your project, whether it's a simple patchwork quilt, a piece of clothing, or a decorative item, you witness the transformation of raw materials into something beautiful and functional. This sense of accomplishment can boost your self-esteem and contribute to a positive outlook on life. In addition to that, this tangible piece you brought to life can also be a souvenir of the years gone by.

Clare Hunter talks about learning to sew with her mother and how it became an essential part of her life, as well as their shared quality time over the years.

"It was my mother who taught me how to sew. She guided me through the simplest of stitches – back stitch, blanket stitch, lazy daisy, French knots – and, through them, I discovered another way of writing, inscribing my cloth with motifs and patterns that seemed to speak of an elsewhere, a world more delicate than the rough and tumble of my own," says the author of Threads of Life: a History of the World Through the Eye of a Needle in her [blog](#).

She further adds, *"When my sister and I sat with our dying mother for four days and nights, I sewed. Although, by that time, she was in a coma, I like to believe she sensed our presence, heard me describing my work-in-progress, and acknowledging the skill she had passed on to me. I still have the cloth I embroidered then. It evokes our last days together, connects me to her still, and gives me comfort. This is the healing power of sewing: a way to express, sometimes exorcise, pain using a tactile language scripted by a needle and thread."*

As we journey deeper into the therapeutic landscape of sewing, we will uncover the ways in which this craft positively influences your mental health, reduces stress, and fosters emotional well-being. It's an opportunity to reconnect with yourself, find tranquility in creativity, and nurture your mind.

Statistics on the Benefits of Sewing for Mental Health

In the world of mental health and well-being, scientific inquiry is an essential compass guiding us toward practices and therapies that can truly make a difference in our lives.

According to a research by NHS England, approximately 25% of adults are eligible to experience at least one identifiable mental health issue within a year. Individuals from various backgrounds may be impacted at different stages of their lives. Mental health challenges stand as the primary contributor to disability in the UK.

In another research by NHS England, 18.0% of children aged 7-16 had a probable mental disorder in 2022, up from 12.1% in 2017. Among those aged 17-19, 10.1% had a probable mental disorder in 2017, rising to 25.7% in 2022.

While it is crucial to get the necessary professional help required to address these issues, there are also some precautionary steps we can take to reduce the chances of experiencing these mental health issues.

The University of Bristol's research initiative, Stitching-Obsession-Wellness, aims to delve into the therapeutic role of sewing within 19th-century asylums as well as its importance to contemporary wellbeing. The significance of this connection has become even more apparent amid the Covid-19 pandemic. Throughout the lockdown period, a substantial number of individuals turned to or revisited sewing as a coping mechanism for the challenges of confined life, as evidenced by Hobbycraft's reported surge of 200% in online sales. Beyond being a mere pastime, sewing has gained recognition for its therapeutic advantages.

Amid a lockdown scenario that intensified existing mental health issues while concurrently witnessing a decrease in mental health services due to staff redirection to the frontline, online sessions and communities centered around "sewing-as-therapy" have thrived. These initiatives provide an accessible means to address and promote mental health and wellness, as observed in projects like Crafting During Coronavirus or Sewing Through the Pandemic.

However, the research also revealed that "sewing-as-therapy" is not a contemporary concept or practice. It was actively endorsed and implemented at Glenside Hospital in the 19th century, formerly known as Bristol Lunatic Asylum (BLA), established in 1861. The hospital, founded on the principles of Moral Treatment, believed that an orderly life could aid the recovery of a disordered mind. In addition to a nourishing diet, the institution provided rest, safety, and occupation, emphasizing useful work as a crucial aspect of treatment. This concept of the therapeutic properties of work echoed the sentiments of Samuel Tuke, the founder of the York Retreat (1796) and an early advocate of mental health reform. In 1861, half of the female patients at BLA were engaged in work, with the majority involved in sewing, encompassing dressmaking, mending, and even some 'fancy sewing'. Examination of patients' medical reports reveals that "Working well at her sewing" served as an indicator of improvement.

Numerous studies have shed light on the therapeutic properties of sewing, unveiling a number of benefits that extend far beyond the stitches and fabric. One of the key findings in this realm is the ability of sewing to induce a state of relaxation. The rhythmic and repetitive nature of sewing acts as a natural tranquilizer, reducing stress levels and promoting a sense of calm.

Clare Hunter shares this sentiment, as she states, *"Sewing is increasingly becoming recognised as an effective way to combat depression, the absorption demanded by needlework – its flow – calming the mind and reducing stress. The sense of accomplishment can boost mental health and improve our immune system, as relief from the pressure of multitasking is replaced by focusing on one thing."*

Research has shown that engaging in activities like sewing can lower cortisol, the hormone associated with stress, which can be particularly beneficial for individuals grappling with anxiety or high-stress lifestyles.

Furthermore, sewing has been linked to improved cognitive function. The intricate problem-solving and decision-making involved in sewing projects stimulate the brain, enhancing its ability to focus and make creative decisions. This cognitive engagement can be especially valuable for those seeking respite from the constant distractions of our digital age.

Additionally, sewing can also slow down cognitive decline as you age.

There is a surprisingly close connection between motor skills and cognitive abilities. While sewing may not initially seem like a physically demanding endeavor, it has the potential to significantly benefit an aging loved one by improving their physical and cognitive capacities. Sewing, irrespective of the technique, inherently refines your hand-eye coordination, thereby indirectly contributing to the preservation of cognitive functions.

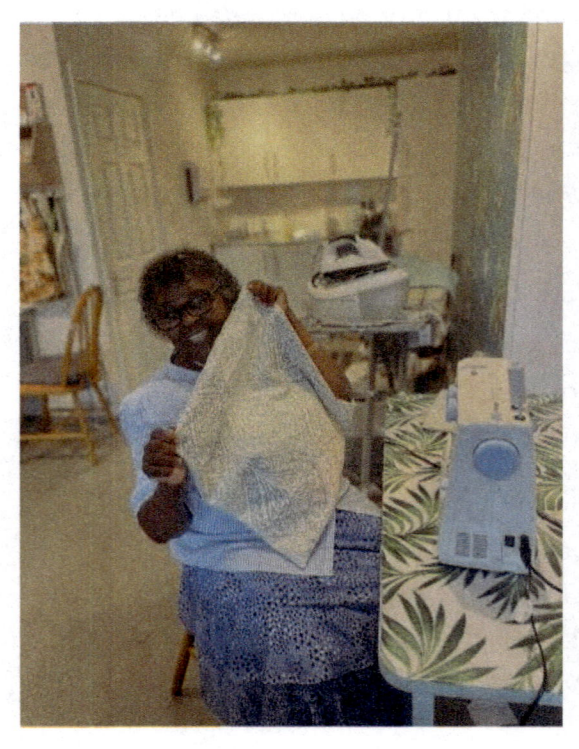

The act of sewing engages an array of motor skills, subtly stimulating the brain while fine-tuning the body's coordination. This practice is invaluable, especially during retirement years, as it offers a dual advantage, providing the aforementioned benefits of boosting motor skills and preventing cognitive decline.

By sewing during retirement, an older adult embarks on a journey that goes beyond the creation of beautiful projects. They embark on a path that strengthens their mental health, potentially lowering the risk of conditions such as Alzheimer's disease and various forms of dementia. In essence, sewing becomes a path to improved cognition and the preservation of a vital mental acumen, contributing to the overall well-being of an older adult.

Studies have also highlighted the role of sewing in boosting self-esteem and self-worth. The act of creating something with your own hands, no matter how small or intricate, fosters a sense of accomplishment. This sense of achievement can significantly impact how you perceive yourself, helping to build a more positive self-image and reinforcing a belief in your abilities.

It is important to note that starting any new venture can be intimidating, and sewing is no exception. For those with little to no experience, the prospect of handling needles, thread, and fabric can be rather daunting. The fear of not being skilled or talented enough, as well as the fear of making mistakes can act as significant obstacles on the path to picking up this craft.

It's perfectly normal to feel apprehensive when venturing into uncharted territory. The idea of not excelling immediately, of not creating flawless stitches or perfectly tailored garments, can be paralyzing. As a result, it can have a negative effect on one's self-esteem. However, it's essential to recognize that these fears, while natural, need not hold you back.

In fact, sewing offers a unique opportunity to confront these fears head-on and transform them into sources of personal growth and self-esteem. It's a journey that teaches us that perfection is not the goal. Rather, it's about embracing the process, learning from every stitch, and realizing that the act of creating, regardless of the outcome, is a triumph in itself.

When you take that first step, when you muster the courage to thread your needle and make that initial stitch, you're already on the path to overcoming your fears. Each stitch shows your willingness to try something new, to challenge yourself, and to persevere despite initial setbacks.

With each project, you'll find your skills improving, your confidence growing, and your self-esteem receiving a significant boost. Sewing teaches you patience, resilience, and the art of self-compassion. You'll realize that it's okay to make mistakes, for they are stepping stones on the path to mastery.

Remember, you don't need to achieve perfection to reap the benefits of sewing. The key is taking that first step, facing your fears, and embracing the process of learning and creating. As you continue to practice, you'll not only witness tangible improvements in your sewing skills but also experience a profound transformation in your self-esteem. So, don't let fear hold you back; instead, let it propel you forward on a journey of personal growth through sewing. And as you keep going, you will see how you'll shine brighter than ever before.

The Biological Effects of Sewing: Dopamine, Serotonin, and Oxytocin

Sewing is more than just a creative pastime; it's a natural mood enhancer that can have profound effects on our biological and emotional well-being. In this section, we'll explore the fascinating connection between sewing and our brain's chemistry, delving into the release of three key neurochemicals: dopamine, serotonin, and oxytocin.

These neurotransmitters, often referred to as the "feel-good" chemicals, play crucial roles in regulating our emotions, mood, and overall mental health. Understanding how sewing triggers the release of these neurochemicals offers us valuable insights into why this craft has such a positive impact on our mental and emotional well-being.

- **Dopamine: The Pleasure Neurotransmitter**

Dopamine is a neurotransmitter associated with pleasure, reward, and motivation. It's often released when we experience something enjoyable or satisfying. When you engage in sewing, especially when you successfully complete a project or achieve a stitching milestone, your brain responds by releasing dopamine. This surge of pleasure reinforces your sense of accomplishment and contributes to the feeling of happiness and contentment associated with sewing.

- **Serotonin: The Mood Regulator**

Serotonin is another neurotransmitter that plays a crucial role in regulating mood, sleep, and appetite. Sewing can lead to an increase in serotonin levels, promoting a sense of relaxation and overall well-being. This is particularly valuable for individuals dealing with stress, anxiety, or mild depressive symptoms. Sewing can act as a natural mood regulator, helping to alleviate negative emotions and improve mental clarity.

- **Oxytocin: The Bonding Hormone**

Oxytocin, often referred to as the "bonding hormone" or "love hormone," is released during social interactions, physical touch, and nurturing activities. When you engage in sewing, you experience a tactile connection with fabrics and textures. This sensory experience can trigger the release of oxytocin, promoting feelings of comfort and connection. Sewing can be a means of self-nurturing and self-care, fostering a sense of emotional well-being and reducing feelings of isolation or loneliness.

Stitch 2: Getting Started with Sewing

The decision to begin this journey of creativity, mindfulness, and self-discovery through sewing is a beautiful step forward. As you delve deeper into the world of sewing, you'll find that it's not just a craft; it's a transformative experience waiting to unfold. This chapter marks the beginning of your exciting adventure - a guide to help you take those crucial first steps into the art of sewing.

Skills for Successful Sewing

Sewing may appear to be a complex skill at first glance, with its array of tools, techniques, and terminology. It's perfectly normal to feel a sense of wonder and perhaps a touch of apprehension as you stand at the threshold of this creative endeavor. But fear not, for this chapter is your compass, your trusted companion, and your gentle mentor as you set out on this path.

In the pages that follow, we'll begin by breaking down the essentials of sewing. You'll discover the fundamental tools and materials you need to get started. From choosing the right fabric and thread to understanding the importance of various sewing notions, we'll lay the groundwork for your sewing journey.

As we progress, we'll delve into the basics of hand sewing and machine sewing. You'll learn the essential stitches, seams, and techniques that form the building blocks of sewing projects. Whether you're brand new to sewing or looking to refresh your skills, these foundational lessons will provide you with the knowledge and confidence to move forward.

But this chapter is not just about acquiring technical skills; it's about embracing the joy of creation. You'll explore the world of patterns, fabrics, and designs, allowing your imagination to take flight. We'll discuss the importance of selecting projects that resonate with you, projects that speak to your heart and inspire your creativity.

Moreover, this chapter serves as an invitation to practice. You'll find practical exercises and tips to hone your skills and build your confidence. Remember, sewing is not about achieving perfection from the start; it's about taking action and relishing the journey of self-improvement.

By the end of this chapter, you'll have taken your first steps into the enchanting world of sewing. You'll have acquired the knowledge, tools, and enthusiasm to begin your creative endeavors with confidence. As you embark on this adventure, remember that every stitch, every project, and every moment spent sewing is a step closer to discovering the incredible therapeutic potential of this timeless craft.

So, let's thread our needles, choose our fabrics, and set forth on this exciting journey of creativity, mindfulness, and self-expression through sewing. The world of sewing awaits, and the possibilities are boundless.

Essential Sewing Tools and Materials

Sewing, like any craft, requires a set of essential tools and materials to bring your creative projects to life. Whether you're a beginner or a seasoned seamstress, having the right equipment at your disposal is crucial. In this section, we'll explore the key tools and materials that will serve as the foundation for your sewing journey.

1. Sewing Machine or Hand Sewing Supplies

Sewing Machine (for Machine Sewing): If you're eager to explore the efficiency and versatility of machine sewing, investing in a good-quality sewing machine is essential. Research different types of sewing machines, considering factors such as your budget, the types of projects you plan to undertake, and the features that suit your needs.

Always make sure to thoroughly go through the instruction manual provided with your sewing machine.

Hand Sewing Supplies (for Hand Sewing): If you prefer the meditative and precise art of hand sewing, gather these basic hand sewing supplies: high-quality needles in various sizes, a thimble to protect your finger while pushing the needle through fabric, and a pair of sharp fabric scissors.

2. Fabric and Thread Selection

Fabric: Choosing the right fabric is crucial for the success of your sewing projects. Familiarize yourself with different fabric types, such as cotton, linen, silk, denim, and more. Each fabric has its unique characteristics, weight, and drape, making it suitable for specific types of projects. Consider the project's purpose, and select a fabric that complements your design and desired functionality.

Thread: High-quality thread is the lifeline of your sewing projects. It's essential to match the thread to your fabric. Understand the different types of threads available, including polyester, cotton, silk, and more. Pay attention to the thread's color, thickness (denier), and whether it's suitable for machine or hand sewing.

3. Cutting and Measuring Tools

Fabric Scissors: A pair of sharp fabric scissors is indispensable for precise cutting. It's essential to reserve these scissors exclusively for fabric to maintain their sharpness.

Pins and Pincushion: Straight pins are essential for holding fabric pieces together before sewing. A pincushion will keep your pins organized and within easy reach.

Measuring Tools: Invest in measuring tools to ensure your sewing projects are accurate and well-fitted:

- **Flexible Measuring Tape:** This is essential for taking body measurements and measuring fabric. Look for one with both metric and imperial measurements.

- **Acrylic Ruler:** A clear acrylic ruler with marked measurements is ideal for measuring and marking fabric for straight cuts and seams. It provides a straight edge for precise cutting and measuring.
- **Right-Angle Ruler:** This tool, also known as a quilting ruler, comes in handy for achieving perfect right angles and precise corners in your sewing projects.

4. Marking and Tracing Tools

Marking your fabric properly is crucial for achieving professional results in sewing. These tools will help you transfer pattern markings and measurements onto your fabric:

Tailor's Chalk: This chalk comes in various colors and is easily visible on most fabrics. It's perfect for marking temporary guidelines.

Fabric Markers and Pens: These come in different types, including washable, disappearing, and heat-erasable markers. Choose the type that best suits your project and fabric.

Pins and Needles: Aside from holding fabric layers together, pins and needles can be useful for basting and securing seams before permanent stitching.

5. Seam Ripper

Mistakes happen in sewing, and a seam ripper is your go-to tool for correcting them. It helps you remove stitches without damaging the fabric. A good-quality seam ripper with a sharp blade is essential.

6. Iron and Ironing Board

Proper pressing and ironing are essential for achieving polished sewing results. Invest in a steam iron with adjustable temperature settings and a sturdy ironing board. Pressing your fabric before sewing helps flatten seams, set creases, and ensure a professional finish to your projects.

These essential sewing tools and materials lay the foundation for your creative journey. Whether you're drawn to hand sewing or eager to explore the possibilities of machine sewing, having the right equipment and materials at your disposal will set you on a path toward successful and enjoyable sewing projects. As you progress in your sewing skills, you may expand your collection to include more specialized tools based on your unique preferences and the projects you undertake.

Remember, the quality of your tools and materials can greatly enhance your sewing experience and the final outcome of your creations. So, gather your supplies so we can embark on this exciting journey of sewing creativity together.

Setting Up Your Sewing Space

A well-organized and dedicated sewing space can greatly enhance your sewing experience and creativity. Whether you have a spacious sewing room or a small corner in your home, optimizing your sewing space is essential for efficiency and enjoyment. In this section, we'll explore the key considerations and tips for setting up a functional and inspiring sewing area.

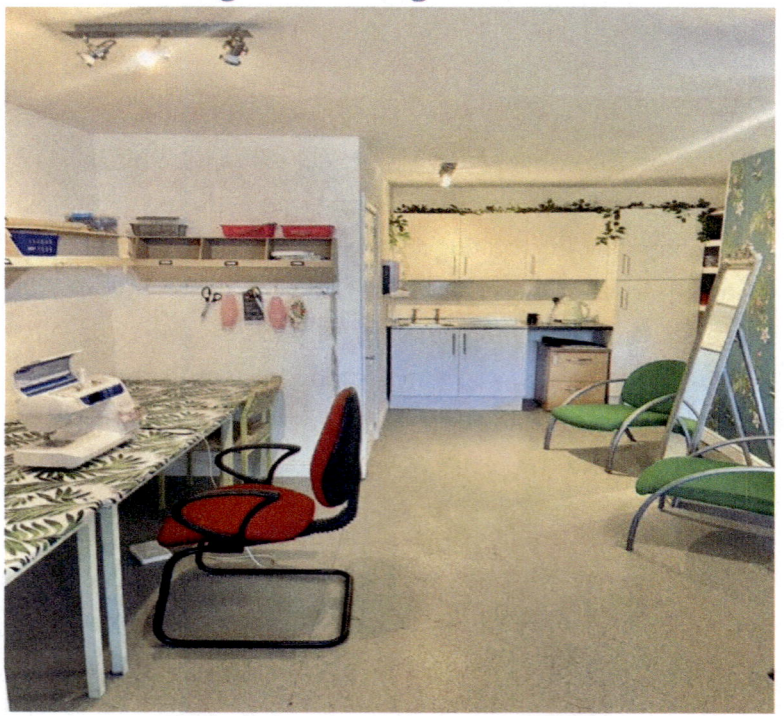

1. Choosing Your Sewing Location

Selecting the right location for your sewing space is the first step. Here are some factors to consider:

Natural Light: Whenever possible, choose a space with ample natural light. Good lighting is crucial for accurate cutting, sewing, and fabric selection.

Accessibility: Ensure your sewing area is easily accessible and doesn't disrupt the flow of your daily activities. Consider proximity to utilities like power outlets and water sources for ironing.

Comfort: Opt for a comfortable, ergonomically sound chair and table height to prevent discomfort and strain during long sewing sessions.

2. **Sewing Furniture and Storage**

Invest in sewing furniture and storage solutions to keep your supplies organized and accessible:

Sewing Table: A sturdy sewing table with a large work surface and adjustable height options is ideal. Some sewing tables come with built-in storage, which can be convenient.

Storage Units: Consider cabinets, drawers, shelves, or wall-mounted storage solutions to keep your fabric, notions, and tools organized. Transparent containers or labeled bins can make it easy to locate specific items.

Thread Rack: A thread rack or organizer can keep your thread spools visible and within reach.

Cutting Mat and Rotary Cutter: Designate a cutting area with a self-healing mat and rotary cutter if space allows.

3. Organizing Your Supplies

Efficient organization is key to a tidy and functional sewing space:

Categorize Supplies: Group your sewing supplies by category, such as fabric, thread, notions, and tools. Store them in labeled containers or drawers for easy access.

Wall Organization: Utilize wall space with pegboards, hooks, or shelves to hang tools and frequently used items.

Clear Containers: Store small items like buttons, zippers, and needles in clear containers to quickly identify contents.

4. Lighting

Proper lighting is essential for accurate sewing:

Task Lighting: Invest in task lighting, such as adjustable desk lamps or overhead lights, to illuminate your work area. LED daylight bulbs are an excellent choice for accurate color matching.

5. Electrical and Sewing Machine Setup

Ensure your sewing area is equipped for your sewing machine and other electrical needs:

Power Outlets: Have sufficient power outlets near your sewing machine and ironing area to avoid using extension cords.

Surge Protector: Use a surge protector to safeguard your sewing machine and other electronic devices from power surges.

6. Personal Touches

Make your sewing space an inviting and inspiring place to create:

Decor and Inspiration: Add personal touches like artwork, inspirational quotes, or a vision board to create a motivating and enjoyable atmosphere.

Comfort: Include cozy elements like cushions, curtains, or rugs to enhance the comfort and aesthetics of your space.

Setting up your sewing space thoughtfully and efficiently ensures you can focus on your creative projects without unnecessary distractions. A well-organized sewing area not only boosts your productivity but also creates an inspiring environment where you can fully immerse yourself in the joy of sewing. So, take the time to organize and personalize your sewing area - it's the first tangible step toward a rewarding and fulfilling sewing journey.

Basic Sewing Techniques for Beginners

On your sewing journey, mastering fundamental sewing techniques is the key to unlocking your creative potential. Whether you're a complete novice or looking to refresh your skills, this section will guide you through the essential sewing techniques that form the building blocks of sewing projects.

These techniques will provide you with the knowledge and confidence to tackle a wide range of sewing projects with ease.

1) Threading Your Needle

Threading a needle may seem like a simple task, but it's a fundamental skill that requires practice. Follow these steps:

- Cut a length of thread (usually about 18 inches) and trim the end to create a clean edge.
- Hold the needle in one hand and the thread in the other.
- Gently moisten the tip of the thread with your lips or a damp sponge.
- Insert the moistened end of the thread through the needle's eye, pulling it through until you have an even tail.

2) Knotting the Thread

Creating a knot at the end of your thread secures it during sewing. Here's how:

- After threading the needle, hold the threaded end and form a loop with the unthreaded end.
- Pass the needle through the loop, creating a small knot at the end of the thread.
- Tighten the knot by pulling both ends gently.

3) Hand Stitches

Hand stitches are the foundation of hand sewing. These are some common hand stitches:

Running Stitch:

The running stitch is one of the simplest and most fundamental hand stitches in sewing. It's often the first stitch beginners learn, and it serves as the foundation for many other stitches and sewing techniques.

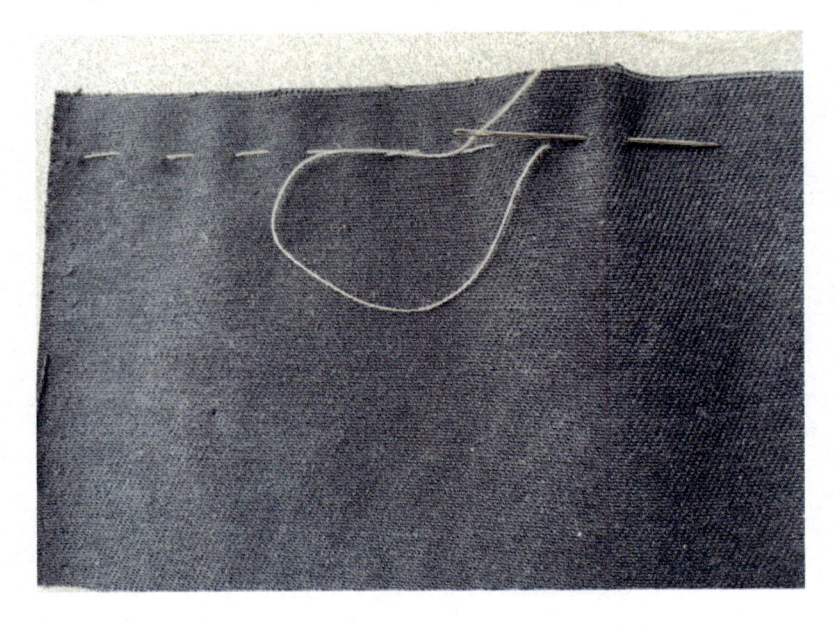

This versatile stitch is used for various purposes, such as basting, gathering, and creating simple seams.

Step-by-Step Guide:

1) Place the two pieces of fabric you want to join together, with the right sides facing each other.

The right side is the side of the fabric you want to show on the finished project.

2) Start the stitch by inserting the needle from the backside (the wrong side) of the fabric, pushing it up through the fabric layers to the front side. The point where the needle comes up is where your first stitch will begin.
3) Push the needle back down through the fabric, about 1/8 to 1/4 inch away from where it came up.
4) Ensure that the stitch length is consistent and matches your desired seam allowance. A common seam allowance is 1/2 inch, so you want to aim for stitches about 1/2 inch apart.
5) Repeat the process of bringing the needle up and down through the fabric, creating evenly spaced stitches along the seam line.
6) As you work, keep the stitches taut but not overly tight. This ensures that the seam is secure without puckering the fabric.
7) When you reach the end of your seam or project, create a knot to secure the thread. You can do this by making a small loop with your last stitch and passing the needle through it before pulling it tight.
8) Trim any excess thread, leaving a short tail.

The simplicity of this stitch makes it an excellent starting point for beginners, and as you gain experience, you'll find various applications for this essential sewing technique.

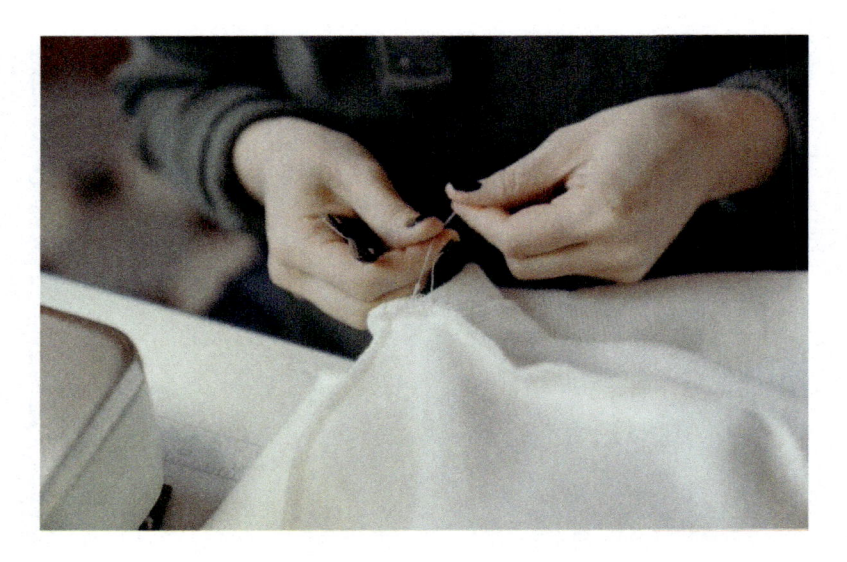

Backstitch:

The backstitch is a strong and versatile hand stitch used in sewing to create secure and durable seams. It's especially valuable when you need extra reinforcement, such as in the construction of garments or items that will undergo stress.

The backstitch involves stitching backward into the previous stitch, creating a continuous line of stitches that's both sturdy and visually appealing.

Step-by-Step Guide

1) Follow the first two steps of the Running Stitch.
2) Instead of immediately pulling the needle back down through the fabric, bring it backward slightly and insert it back into the same hole from which it came up. This creates the first half of your backstitch.
3) Pull the needle and thread through the fabric until the stitch is snug but not overly tight.
4) Now, move your needle forward, away from the last stitch, and insert it into the fabric, creating a small stitch.
5) Pull the needle through to the front side of the fabric.
6) To create the backstitch, repeat the process. After inserting the needle into the fabric ahead of the

previous stitch, bring it backward, and then insert it into the same hole as the previous stitch.
7) Continue this process of stitching forward, then backward, keeping the stitches evenly spaced and tight. This creates a strong and secure line of stitching.
8) Just like the running stitch, end the backstitch by creating a knot to secure the thread and trim any excess thread.

The backstitch is a valuable technique for creating strong and durable seams in sewing projects. With practice, you'll become proficient in creating neat and secure backstitches, adding a professional touch to your sewing projects.

Basting Stitch:

The basting stitch is a long, temporary hand stitch used in sewing to hold fabric layers together temporarily. It's particularly useful when you need to secure fabric before permanent stitching, make fitting adjustments, or create gathers. Basting stitches are easy to remove when they're no longer needed, making them an essential technique in sewing.

<u>Step-by-Step Guide</u>

1) Follow the first two steps of the Running Stitch.

2) Create a long stitch by moving the needle forward, away from the last stitch, and inserting it into the fabric ahead of the previous stitch.
3) Pull the needle through to the front side of the fabric. The resulting stitch should be longer than typical sewing stitches.
4) Repeat the process of making long, evenly-spaced stitches. These stitches should be long enough to hold the fabric layers together securely but loose enough that they can be easily removed when needed.
5) Avoid pulling the thread too tightly, as you want the stitches to be easily removable.
6) Just like the previous stitches, end the basting stitch by creating a knot to secure the thread and trim any excess thread.

The basting stitch is a valuable technique for various sewing applications. It allows you to temporarily secure fabric layers for fitting adjustments, gathering fabric, or ensuring that seams align correctly before permanent stitching. When your sewing project reaches the point where the basting stitches are no longer needed, they can be easily removed by gently pulling on the thread, leaving your fabric ready for final stitching and finishing.

Whipstitch:

The whipstitch is a basic hand-sewing stitch that is easy to learn and incredibly versatile. It's used for joining two fabric edges together, making it a valuable technique in various sewing projects. Whether you're closing seams, attaching patches, or creating simple seams in crafts, the whipstitch is a go-to stitch for many sewists.

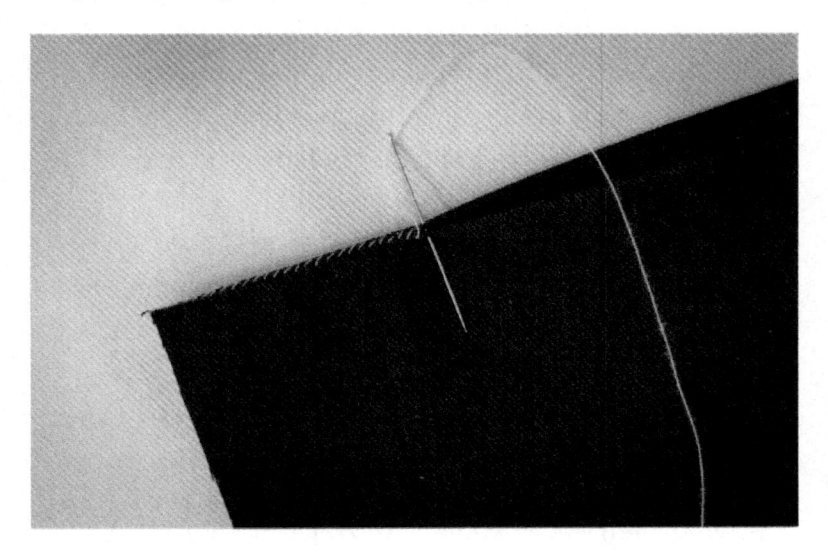

Step-by-Step Guide

1) Place the two pieces of fabric you want to join together, aligning the edges you want to sew. Ensure that the right sides (the sides of the fabric you want to show on the finished project) are facing each other.
2) Insert the needle from the backside (the wrong side) of the fabric, pushing it up through the bottom layer of fabric to the front side, near the edge. The point where the needle comes up is where your first whipstitch will begin.

3) Move the needle diagonally, from right to left (or left to right), inserting it into the top layer of fabric. This diagonal motion creates a slanted stitch.
4) Pull the needle and thread through, leaving a small loop of thread on the surface.
5) Repeat the process by moving the needle diagonally in the same direction, inserting it into the top layer of fabric, and pulling it through to create another slanted stitch.
6) Keep the stitches evenly spaced and snug but not overly tight. The diagonal stitches should be close together, forming a neat seam.
7) Similar to the previous stitches, end the basting stitch by creating a knot to secure the thread and trim any excess thread.

The whipstitch is a versatile and straightforward stitch used in various sewing and crafting applications. It's often used for closing seams in soft toys, pillows, and quilting, as well as attaching appliqué pieces and patches to fabric.

Blind Hem Stitch:

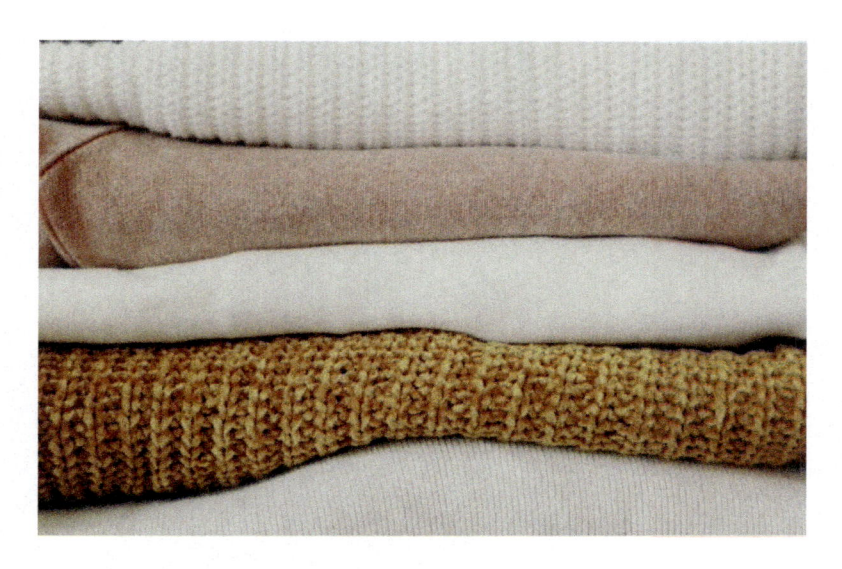

The blind hem stitch is a sewing technique used to create a nearly invisible hem on garments, curtains, or other fabric items. It's a useful method for achieving a clean, finished look without visible stitches on the outside of the fabric. This stitch is often used in professional sewing and tailoring to create hems that appear seamless.

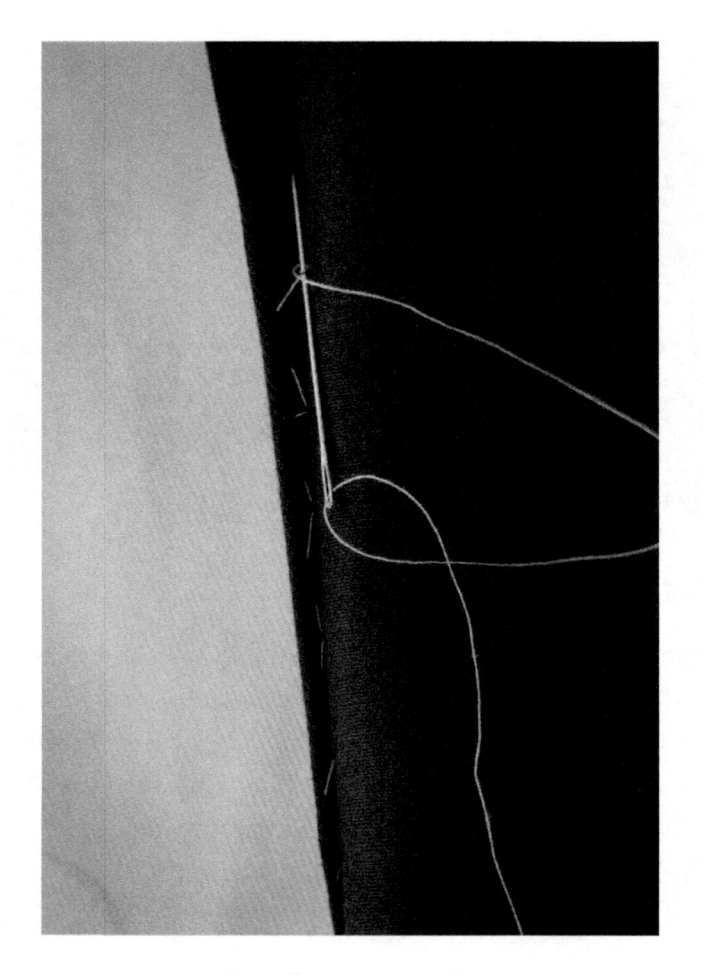

Step-by-Step Guide

1) Begin by folding and pressing the fabric to create the desired hem. The folded edge should align with the fabric's wrong side, leaving the right side exposed. Position the fabric with the folded edge facing you.

2) Insert the needle from the inside of the folded edge, bringing it out to the right side of the fabric. The point where the needle comes out is where your first blind hem stitch will begin.
3) To create the first stitch, insert the needle into the folded edge (inside the hem) about 0.25cm and 0.5cm away from the starting point.
4) Bring the needle out to the right side of the fabric, making sure it catches a small amount of fabric from the folded edge.
5) As you continue stitching, insert the needle into the folded edge (inside the hem) about 1/4 inch away from the previous stitch.
6) Bring the needle out to the right side, again catching a small amount of fabric from the folded edge.
7) The key to the blind hem stitch's invisibility is to keep the stitches small and evenly spaced. The stitches should be barely visible on the right side of the fabric.
8) Repeat the process of inserting the needle into the folded edge, spacing the stitches about 1/4 inch apart until you reach the end of the hem.
9) Once you reach the end of your hem, secure the thread by making a small knot on the inside of the folded edge. This knot should be hidden within the hem.

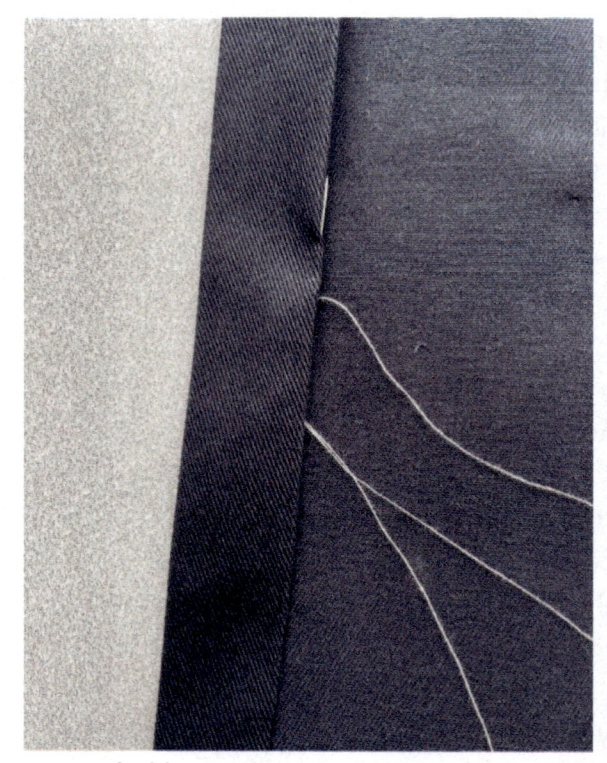

The blind hem stitch creates an almost invisible hem on your fabric, making it an excellent choice for garments with delicate or sheer fabrics. With practice, you can achieve perfectly concealed hems that give your sewing projects a polished and professional appearance.

Seam Allowance

Understanding and maintaining seam allowance is crucial for accurate sewing. Seam allowance is the distance between the stitching line and the fabric edge. A common seam allowance is 0.5 to 1 cm, but it can vary depending on your project and pattern. So please allow

Pressing Seams

Properly pressing seams is a key step in achieving polished sewing results. Always press seams flat before and after stitching. Follow these steps:

- Set your iron to the appropriate temperature for your fabric.
- Place the seam on the ironing board with the fabric's wrong side facing up.
- Gently press the iron onto the seam, moving it along the length to ensure a flat, crisp seam.

Clipping and Notching

These are techniques used to reduce bulk and allow seams to lie flat. Here's how they work:

Clipping:

Clipping involves making small, straight cuts into the seam allowance of fabric, typically at points where the fabric curves or folds. It is used to allow the fabric to ease into a curve or corner without creating wrinkles or puckers. Clipping is essential for achieving a neat and smooth finish, especially when sewing garments or curved seams.

1) Before you start sewing, identify the areas where you'll need to clip. These are typically curves,

48

corners, or any areas where the seam allowance needs to adapt to the shape of the fabric.
2) First, sew the seam as instructed in your pattern, but do not sew into the seam allowance where you plan to clip.
3) Once the seam is sewn, take your scissors and carefully trim any excess seam allowance to reduce bulk. Leave about 1/8 to 1/4 of seam allowance.
4) To clip, make small, straight cuts perpendicular to the seam line, and stop just before reaching the stitching. These cuts should be spaced evenly and extend into the seam allowance.
5) The spacing of your clips depends on the curvature of the seam. For gentle curves, you may space the clips further apart, while tighter curves require closer spacing.
6) Be cautious not to cut too close to the seam, as you don't want to cut through the stitching accidentally.
7) After clipping, test the curve by gently pressing the seam open or to one side, depending on your project. The clipped areas will allow the fabric to ease into the curve without causing tension or puckering.

Notching:

Notching is another technique used to reduce bulk in seams, especially in areas where the fabric curves or forms corners. Notches involve cutting small triangular or Vshaped sections out of the seam allowance. This process helps the fabric to lie flat and creates a smoother, more professional finish.

1) Like clipping, notching should be done before sewing the seam. Identify the areas where notches are needed, typically curves, corners, or areas with a lot of seam allowance.
2) Begin by sewing the seam, but do not sew into the areas where you plan to notch.
3) After sewing, trim any excess seam allowance, leaving about 1/8 to 1/4 inch.
4) To create a notch, make small, triangular cuts into the seam allowance. These cuts should extend from the edge of the seam allowance and stop just short of the stitching line.
5) Space the notches based on the curvature of the seam. Tighter curves may require more closely

spaced notches, while gentler curves may need fewer notches.
6) After notching, remove any remaining excess fabric in the corners to further reduce bulk.
7) Gently press the seam open or to one side. The notches will allow the fabric to lie flat and conform to the curve or corner without creating folds or wrinkles.

Both clipping and notching are essential techniques for achieving a clean and professional finish in sewing projects. They help ensure that seams lie flat and smooth, especially in areas with curves or corners, and are crucial for creating well-fitted garments and other fabric items.

Finishing Seams

Finishing seams is an important step in sewing to prevent fraying, reduce bulk, and create a neat and professional look on the inside of your garments or fabric projects.

The method you choose for finishing seams depends on the type of fabric you're working with and your project's requirements.

Here are some common methods for finishing seams:

Zigzag Stitch:

- On a regular sewing machine, set it to a zigzag stitch.

- Sew along the edge of the seam allowance, allowing the zigzag stitch to encase the raw edge of the fabric.
- Trim any excess fabric close to the zigzag stitching.
- This method works well for medium-weight fabrics and prevents fraying.

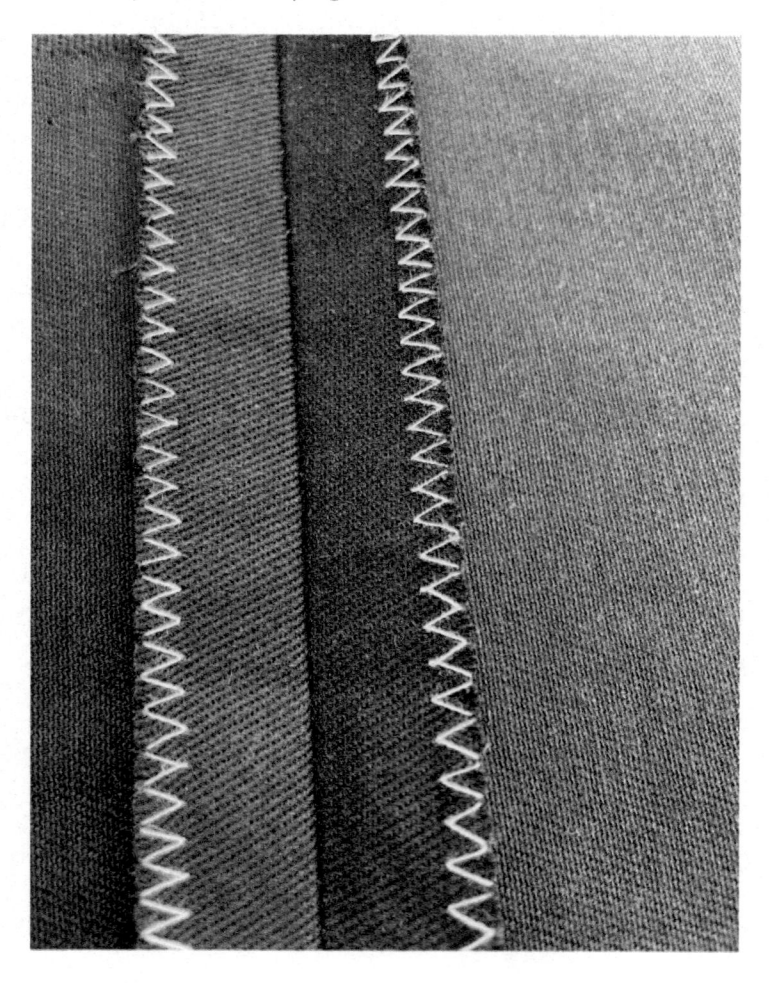

Overlock or Serger Machine:

- If you have access to an overlock or serger machine, it's an excellent choice for seam finishing.
- Run the edge of your fabric through the serger, which will trim the excess fabric and overcast the edge.

This method is ideal for most fabric types, including lightweight and heavy fabrics.

French Seam:

- Start by sewing the seam with the wrong sides together. Trim the seam allowance, press it flat, and then fold the fabric so that the right sides are together.
- Sew a second seam, encasing the raw edge of the first seam.

A French seam is a more advanced finishing technique that encases the raw edge of the seam for a clean and polished look. This method works well for lightweight and delicate fabrics.

<u>Bound Seam:</u>

- To create a bound seam, cut a strip of fabric (bias tape or selvage strips work well) and fold it in half with the wrong sides together.
- Open the seam allowance, place the folded strip along the seam allowance, and stitch it in place.

This method is excellent for decorative finishes and heavy fabrics.

Hemming Tape or Fusible Web:

56

- Hemming tape or fusible web can be used to finish seams in lightweight fabrics.
- Place the tape or web along the raw edge of the seam allowance and press it with an iron to fuse it in place.

This method is quick and easy but may not be as durable as other methods.

Serged and Folded Seam (Clean Finish):

- On a regular sewing machine, sew the seam as usual.
- Trim the seam allowance to about 1/4 inch.
- Fold one edge of the seam allowance under, enclosing the raw edge, and sew a second seam to secure the fold.

This method creates a clean and durable finish and works well for lightweight to medium-weight fabrics.

The choice of seam finishing method depends on your fabric type, the look you want to achieve, and the sewing equipment available to you. Experiment with different techniques to find the one that suits your project best. Properly finished seams not only prevent fraying but also add durability and a professional touch to your sewing creations.

Your First Sewing Project

Starting your first sewing project can be an exciting and rewarding experience, and it's a great way to apply the skills you've learned. Whether you're a complete beginner or someone looking to build on existing knowledge, here is a detailed guide to help you get started with your first sewing project:

Your First Sewing Project: A Step-by-Step Guide
Choose a Simple Project:

For your first project, it's essential to choose something straightforward and achievable. Consider simple sewing projects like a cushion cover, tote bag, or a basic skirt. These projects typically involve straight seams and minimal fabric manipulation.

Gather Your Supplies:

Before you begin, make sure you have all the necessary supplies, including fabric, matching thread, sewing machine (or hand-sewing supplies if you're working by hand), scissors, pins, and any additional notions required for your chosen project.

Select the Fabric:

Choose a fabric that's appropriate for your project. For beginners, it's a good idea to work with medium-weight, woven fabrics like cotton or linen. Avoid fabrics that are too slippery, stretchy, or delicate, as they can be more challenging to sew.

Cut Your Fabric:

Measure and cut your fabric pieces according to the pattern or project instructions. Use a ruler, fabric scissors, and straight pins to ensure accuracy.

Prepare Your Machine:

If you're using a sewing machine, make sure it's threaded correctly with the right color thread and that the needle is appropriate for your fabric. Set your machine to a straight stitch for most beginner projects.

Pinning and Stitching:

Align the fabric pieces with right sides together (if applicable) and pin them in place along the edges to be sewn. Start sewing, keeping a consistent seam allowance (usually 1/2 inch or as specified), and removing pins as you go.

Backstitching and Securing Seams:

At the beginning and end of each seam, use the backstitch function (a few reverse stitches) to secure the seam. This prevents the stitching from unraveling.

Press the Seams:

After sewing, press the seams open or in the direction indicated in your pattern. This step helps your project look neat and professional.

Finish the Edges:

If your project requires it, consider finishing the raw edges of your fabric. You can use pinking shears, a zigzag stitch on your sewing machine, or other seam-finishing techniques mentioned earlier.

Assemble Your Project:

Continue following the pattern or project instructions to assemble your project. This may involve attaching closures (e.g., zippers or buttons) or adding additional details.

Final Pressing and Inspection:

Give your project a final press to ensure it looks its best. Inspect your work for any loose threads or imperfections and make any necessary corrections.

Enjoy Your Completed Project:

Once you've finished your first sewing project, take a moment to admire your work and the skills you've gained. Use or wear your creation with pride, and remember that practice is key to improving your sewing abilities.

Tips for Success:
- Take your time, and don't rush through the steps.
- Read the pattern or project instructions carefully before starting.
- Don't be discouraged by mistakes; they're part of the learning process.
- Practice basic sewing techniques on scrap fabric to build confidence.
- Consider taking a beginner sewing class or watching online tutorials for additional guidance.

Starting your first sewing project is a significant milestone in your sewing journey. It's an opportunity to apply your skills, gain hands-on experience, and create something that's uniquely yours. With each project, you'll build confidence and develop your sewing abilities, paving the way for more complex and rewarding creations in the future.

Stitch 3: The Art of Breathing and Relaxation

In the whirlwind of our modern lives, where the demands of work, family, and technology often consume our every waking moment, it's easy to forget the simple art of taking a deep breath and allowing ourselves to truly relax. We live in an age of constant connectivity and ever-present stressors, and the effects on our mental and physical well-being can be profound.

But within the chaos and demands of our daily routines, there exists a profound yet simple practice that can be a lifeline to tranquility, clarity, and emotional balance - the art of conscious breathing and relaxation.

The journey into the world of sewing for relaxation and well-being isn't just about fabric and stitches; it's a holistic experience that encompasses the interplay between the creative spirit and the serene mind. The act of sewing, with its rhythmic motions and tactile engagement, has the incredible power to soothe our restless minds and heal our weary souls. Paired with the art of conscious breathing and relaxation, this practice becomes a dynamic force for mental and emotional rejuvenation.

This chapter explores the vital relationship between the act of sewing and the practice of deep, intentional breathing and relaxation. We delve into how these activities influence our bodies, from regulating stress hormones to promoting the release of feel-good neurotransmitters. You'll discover how the simple act of sewing becomes a mindful meditation, allowing you to disconnect from the relentless noise of the outside world and reconnect with your inner self.

As you stitch and breathe, you'll find yourself journeying toward a state of inner peace, where the incessant demands of life recede and the world of tranquility unfolds.

The Connection Between Breathing and Well-being

Breathing is an innate and seemingly effortless aspect of our daily lives. With each inhalation and exhalation, we exchange life-sustaining oxygen and release carbon dioxide, a process orchestrated by our autonomic nervous system. While we rarely give it a second thought, the simple act of breathing holds the key to our physical and emotional equilibrium.

Our breath, far from being a mere biological necessity, is a powerful tool that can be harnessed to promote our overall well-being. It's the bridge that connects the physical and mental realms of our existence, capable of influencing our physiological responses and emotional states.

In this section, we will explore the complex and intricate relationship between conscious breathing and the profound impact it can have on our mental and emotional health.

The Power of Breath in Regulating Stress:

Stress is an omnipresent force in our lives, often accompanied by a surge of the stress hormone cortisol. Prolonged exposure to high levels of cortisol can lead to a range of health issues, including anxiety, depression, and a weakened immune system. The simple act of mindful breathing, however, can help regulate cortisol levels and reduce the body's stress response. As you practice deep, intentional breaths, your parasympathetic nervous system is activated, promoting a state of relaxation that counteracts the effects of stress.

Balancing Emotions Through Breathing:

Emotions, both positive and negative, can be influenced by the way we breathe. Shallow, rapid breaths are often associated with anxiety and tension, while slow, deep breaths can induce a sense of calm and tranquility. Through specific breathing techniques, you can gain greater control over your emotional responses. Whether you're seeking to alleviate moments of anxiety or enhance your overall emotional balance, your breath is a powerful ally.

Boosting Cognitive Function:

Oxygen is essential for optimal brain function. The brain requires a consistent supply of oxygen to maintain cognitive performance, including memory, concentration, and decision-making. Deep and deliberate breathing ensures a steady oxygen supply, enhancing cognitive function and mental clarity. As you engage in the act of sewing and focus on your breath, you'll find your mind becoming more attuned and capable.

Promoting Relaxation and Sleep:

One of the most immediate benefits of conscious breathing is its ability to induce relaxation. By controlling your breath and activating the relaxation response, you can ease tension, promote better sleep, and create a peaceful mindset. The connection between relaxation and sleep is profound, as it's during rest that our bodies regenerate and heal. The calming influence of breath can be particularly valuable during times of insomnia or restlessness.

Incorporating Mindfulness into Your Sewing Practice

At its core, mindfulness is about being aware of the present moment without judgment. It involves paying full attention to your thoughts, feelings, and bodily sensations as they arise. When you practice mindfulness, you acknowledge and accept your experiences, cultivating a deep sense of presence and tranquility.

Steps to Incorporating Mindfulness into Your Sewing Practice:

Sewing naturally lends itself to mindfulness. The tactile nature of working with fabric, the rhythmic flow of stitches, and the concentration required for precise craftsmanship create an ideal environment for cultivating mindfulness. The act of sewing compels you to focus entirely on the task at hand, allowing worries and distractions to fade into the background.

Set an Intention:

Start your sewing session with a clear intention to practice mindfulness. Decide that you will be fully present in each stitch, embracing the process with curiosity and acceptance.

Breathe Mindfully:

Begin your sewing by taking a few deep breaths. As you inhale, focus on the sensation of the breath entering your body. Then, release any tension or distraction with every exhale. Use this exercise as an anchor to the present moment.

Engage Your Senses:

Sewing is a sensory experience. Engage your sense of touch as you handle the fabric and guide it through the machine or with your hand. Observe the colors, textures, and patterns in the fabric. Listen to the hum of the sewing machine or the gentle rustle of the fabric as you work.

Observe Thoughts and Emotions:

As you sew, notice any thoughts or emotions that arise. Without judgment, acknowledge them and allow them to pass through your awareness like clouds in the sky. Return your focus to the tactile sensation of sewing.

Appreciate the Journey:

Often, our focus is fixed on the end result, but mindfulness invites you to appreciate the journey itself. Savor the act of stitching, the evolving pattern, and the sense of accomplishment at each step.

Mindfulness Benefits in Sewing:
- The integration of mindfulness into your sewing practice enhances its therapeutic and stress-reducing effects. It allows you to be fully absorbed in the creative process, leading to a state of flow where time seems to stand still. This not only fosters relaxation but also sharpens your attention and concentration.
- Mindful sewing encourages a sense of self-compassion. It reminds you that it's okay to make mistakes and to accept yourself as you are. With this compassionate mindset, sewing becomes an act of self-care and self-expression.
- The practice of mindfulness during sewing extends beyond your creative time, positively impacting your daily life. It can lead to improved mental clarity, emotional resilience, and a greater capacity for managing stress.

Incorporating mindfulness into your sewing practice isn't just about creating beautiful projects; it's about creating a beautiful state of mind. With each stitch, you have the opportunity to cultivate a sense of inner peace, creativity, and acceptance that extends far beyond the sewing room.

As you immerse yourself in the union of sewing and mindfulness, you'll find a path to greater self-awareness, serenity, and a deeper connection to the world around you.

Stitch 4: Nurturing Your Well-being

Sewing, more than a craft or pastime, is a profound practice with the potential to transform your creativity and enhance your overall sense of well-being. This chapter delves into the heart of nurturing your well-being through the therapeutic art of sewing. It's an exploration of the transformative power that sewing offers, welcoming individuals of all backgrounds and experiences to find solace, creativity, and inner balance. Through the interconnected threads of creativity, self-care, and mindfulness, you'll discover how sewing can mend not only fabric but also your mental and emotional health.

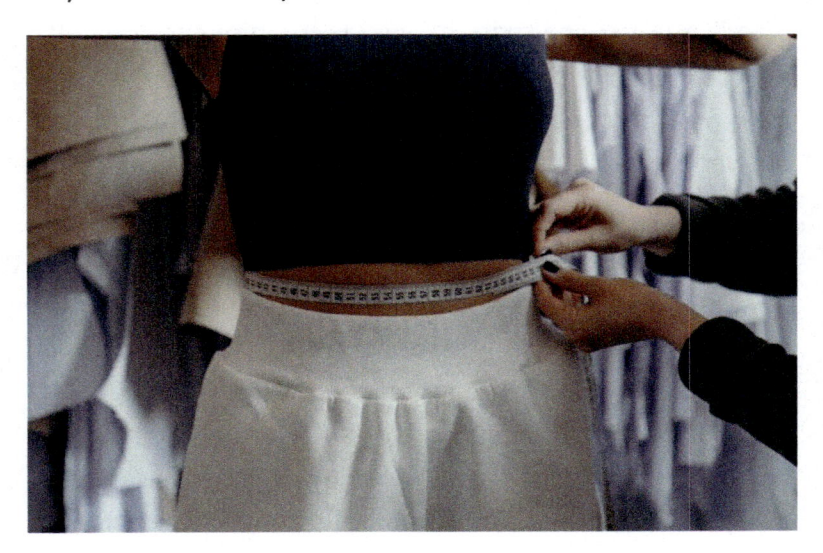

It's a journey that transcends the boundaries of age and experience, offering a path to greater self-awareness, serenity, and a deeper connection with the world around you. Prepare to thread the needle of your creativity and stitch together the fabric of your own well-being, one mindful and self-caring moment at a time.

Self-Care Strategies for Sewists

It is crucial to ensure that your creative pursuits enhance your overall well-being. Here are some self-care strategies tailored for sewists to help you find balance, joy, and relaxation in your sewing practice:

Create a Dedicated Sewing Space:

Designating a specific area for your sewing endeavors can make a world of difference. Whether it's a corner of a room, a spare bedroom, or a well-organized closet, having a dedicated sewing space allows you to immerse yourself in your craft without the constant need to set up and pack away your materials. It also serves as a physical boundary between your creative time and the rest of your daily life.

Prioritize Ergonomics:

Sewing often involves hours of focused work at a sewing machine or hand-sewing station. To prevent physical strain and discomfort, prioritize ergonomics in your sewing setup. Ensure your chair and worktable are at the correct height, position your sewing machine or materials at eye level, and invest in a comfortable chair with good lumbar support. Take short breaks to stretch and relax your body.

Mindful Sewing Practices:

Sewing, when approached with mindfulness, becomes a form of meditation. Practice intentional breathing as you sew, allowing it to calm your mind and anchor you in the present moment. Let go of perfectionism and embrace the creative process with an open heart. Instead of rushing to finish a project, savor each stitch and each moment of creative flow.

Schedule Regular Breaks:

It's easy to lose track of time when you're engrossed in a sewing project. To prevent burnout and maintain your mental and physical health, schedule regular breaks. Set an alarm or use a timer to remind yourself to step away from your work, stretch, hydrate, and rest your eyes. These breaks will help you return to your sewing with renewed focus and energy.

Balance Creative Projects:

As a sewist, you might have a never-ending list of creative ideas and projects you want to tackle. While it's exciting to explore different projects, be mindful of overcommitting. Balance your creative load by focusing on one or two projects at a time, allowing you to fully immerse yourself in each and relish the satisfaction of completing them.

Embrace the Joy of Sharing:

Sewing is often a solitary pursuit, but it doesn't have to be. Consider sharing your creative passion with others. Join a sewing group, attend workshops, or simply engage in conversations with fellow sewists. Sharing your experiences, challenges, and successes with a community of like-minded individuals can be incredibly rewarding and inspiring.

Celebrate Your Achievements:

 Don't forget to acknowledge and celebrate your sewing achievements, no matter how big or small. Completing a project, mastering a new technique, or even just finding time to sew amidst a busy schedule are all worthy of celebration. Recognizing your accomplishments boosts your self-esteem and motivates you to continue your sewing journey with enthusiasm.

By integrating these self-care strategies into your sewing practice, you'll not only enhance your creative experiences but also nurture your overall well-being. Sewing can be a deeply fulfilling and therapeutic endeavor when approached with mindfulness and balance, ensuring that it remains a source of joy, relaxation, and personal growth in your life.

Managing Stress and Anxiety Through Sewing

The act of creating with fabric and thread can be a powerful tool to help manage and alleviate stress and anxiety.

Here's how sewing can serve as an effective stress-reduction and anxiety-management technique:

A Calming Rhythm:

Sewing has an inherent rhythmic quality. The repetitive nature of stitching and the gentle hum of a sewing machine provides a soothing background beat. Engaging with this rhythm can help calm the nervous system and reduce stress. As you focus on your stitches, your mind naturally shifts away from stressful thoughts and into the meditative flow of the creative process.

Mindful Distraction:

Anxiety often involves repetitive and intrusive thoughts. Sewing offers a healthy form of distraction. When you immerse yourself in a sewing project, you direct your attention toward a creative task. This shift in focus allows you to step away from the source of your anxiety temporarily and provides a mental break. The act of creating becomes a mindful practice that encourages living in the present moment.

Achievement and Mastery:

Completing a sewing project provides a sense of accomplishment and mastery. This positive reinforcement can boost self-esteem and self-worth, which are often negatively affected by stress and anxiety. The satisfaction of bringing an idea to life and creating something tangible can be a powerful counterbalance to feelings of inadequacy or helplessness.

Creative Expression:

Sewing offers a unique channel for creative expression. It allows you to translate your thoughts, emotions, and artistic ideas into physical creations. This form of self-expression can be deeply cathartic, enabling you to release pent-up emotions and process the underlying causes of stress and anxiety.

Reducing Physical Tension:

The physical act of sewing can help release muscular tension. As you guide the fabric through a machine or hand-stitch, your hands and body engage in deliberate, controlled movements. This action can reduce physical stress and promote relaxation. Incorporating deep breathing exercises while sewing enhances this relaxation effect.

Fostering Mindfulness:

Mindfulness, the practice of being fully present in the moment without judgment, is a well-established method for reducing stress and anxiety. Sewing naturally lends itself to mindfulness. The tactile sensations, the visual engagement with the fabric, and the deliberate focus on stitches immerse you in the creative process and quiet the mind.

Connection and Community:

Sewing can be a solitary practice, but it also offers opportunities for social engagement. Joining a sewing group or participating in workshops can provide a sense of community and support. Sharing your sewing experiences with others can be a source of encouragement and friendship, which can be instrumental in reducing feelings of isolation and anxiety.

Sewing, when approached as a mindful and intentional practice, can become your refuge in times of stress and anxiety. Whether you're sewing to complete a project or simply to engage with the soothing rhythm of stitches, this creative pursuit offers a safe and nurturing space to find solace and inner calm. By harnessing the therapeutic benefits of sewing, you can proactively manage stress and anxiety, finding peace and resilience amid life's challenges.

Finding Balance in Your Life

In the modern world, the pursuit of balance is often akin to chasing a mirage in the desert - elusive yet essential. The demands of work, family, and daily responsibilities can leave us feeling perpetually stretched and stressed. Sewing, as a practice that encourages mindfulness and creativity, can become a touchstone for restoring balance in your life.

Here's how sewing can help you find equilibrium in the midst of life's hectic pace:

A Time for You:

Sewing offers a dedicated time for self-care, allowing you to prioritize your well-being. This time is not selfish but necessary, as it provides a respite from daily demands and responsibilities. In these moments, you can rediscover a sense of self and self-worth, which are crucial for achieving balance.

Mindful Living:

The practice of sewing encourages mindful living. As you immerse yourself in the creative process, you become attuned to the present moment. This awareness spills over into your daily life, making you more conscious of your choices, actions, and interactions. Mindfulness can help you navigate life's challenges with greater ease and presence.

A Creative Outlet:

Creative expression is an essential component of finding balance. Sewing provides a canvas for your creativity, allowing you to explore, experiment, and express yourself. This outlet becomes a sanctuary where you can release pent-up emotions and foster a sense of emotional equilibrium.

Achievement and Fulfillment:

Setting and achieving sewing goals can bring a sense of accomplishment and fulfillment. These moments of success counterbalance the stresses of daily life and enhance your overall well-being. Celebrating your sewing achievements becomes a means to mark personal growth and progress.

A Pause from Technology:

The pervasive presence of technology in our lives can disrupt our sense of balance. Sewing offers a pause from screens, notifications, and constant connectivity. It allows you to disconnect from the digital world and reconnect with your inner self, fostering a sense of balance between the virtual and physical realms.

Building Boundaries:

By designating specific times for sewing, you're creating boundaries in your life. These boundaries help protect your personal time and well-being, making it easier to find a balance between work, family, and personal pursuits. They signify that it's okay to prioritize self-care.

Self-Expression and Identity:

Sewing is not just about making physical creations; it's about shaping your identity. As you engage in the creative process, you discover more about yourself, your tastes, and your passions. This self-discovery is an integral part of finding balance and alignment in your life.

By integrating sewing into your daily routine and approaching it as a mindful and creative practice, you can restore and maintain a sense of balance. It becomes a sanctuary where you can step away from life's chaos, reflect on your inner self, and find equilibrium. Sewing offers not just the joy of creating but also the joy of rediscovering your sense of balance and fulfillment in an increasingly demanding world.

Stitch 5: Empowerment Through Creativity

Sewing isn't just about making garments, quilts, or home decor; it's about making a statement. It's a declaration of your capacity to create, to shape your world, and to infuse it with your unique perspective. In this journey of empowerment, you'll uncover how sewing can foster self-confidence, resilience, and a sense of achievement that extends far beyond the sewing room.

As you work with fabric, you're not merely crafting practical items; you're unveiling your creative potential.

79

Beyond the stitches and seams, beyond the tangible projects, lies a journey of self-discovery, self-belief, and the liberation of your creative spirit.

Unleashing Your Creative Potential

Sewing, often seen as a practical craft, transcends the mere act of creating garments or home decor. It is a transformative journey that unveils the artist within, providing a canvas for self-expression and a powerful tool for self-empowerment. The world of sewing is an expansive realm where creativity knows no bounds. It invites you to explore, experiment, and express yourself in a tangible, beautiful way. It's a practice that empowers you to not only make beautiful things but also to make a profound statement of self-belief.

At the heart of this creative journey is the exploration of your artistic voice. Sewing is not just about following patterns and instructions; it's about making choices that reflect your individuality. As you sift through an array of fabric choices, select patterns, and decide on color palettes, you're making artistic decisions that echo your unique perspective. Each choice is a brushstroke on the canvas of your sewing project, a reflection of your creative instincts. This process encourages you to explore your own artistic voice and embrace the beauty of your individual perspective.

Sewing is an avenue for self-expression where inspiration can be found everywhere. The colors of a sunset, the textures of nature, the patterns of daily life — these sources of inspiration are boundless. When you encounter the world with a creative eye, you begin to see beauty and potential in the most unexpected places. Sewing empowers you to take these inspirations and bring them to life, to transform abstract ideas into tangible creations that resonate with your heart and your unique style.

Perhaps one of the most liberating aspects of sewing is the joy of experimentation. Creativity thrives on the willingness to try new things and to push the boundaries of what is known and comfortable. Sewing provides the perfect platform for this. Whether you're trying a new embroidery stitch, adapting a vintage pattern for a modern look, or experimenting with fabric textures, sewing invites you to embrace the spirit of adventure. This experimentation is the heartbeat of your sewing journey. It opens the door to unexpected discoveries and personal growth, showing that creativity is not a static concept but a dynamic force of self-expression and empowerment.

The act of turning your ideas into reality is a fundamental aspect of sewing's capacity to empower. It bridges the gap between imagination and tangible creation. When you take a concept in your mind and transform it into a physical sewing project, you're engaging in a profound act of self-empowerment. You're not just dreaming; you're making your dreams come true. Sewing provides a structured path from inception to realization, making your creative ideas concrete and tangible. It demonstrates that creativity is not a fleeting thought but a powerful force capable of manifesting your vision.

Moreover, sewing is a journey of continuous self-improvement. It is an artistic evolution. As you tackle new projects and learn new techniques, you're evolving as an artist. This journey fosters self-confidence and self-belief. It becomes a testament to your capacity for growth and your ability to face creative challenges head-on. Each project represents a new challenge, an opportunity to learn, and a chance to build self-confidence. These moments of growth extend far beyond the sewing room, empowering you to navigate life's challenges with an unwavering sense of self-belief.

In essence, sewing becomes a pathway to empowerment through creativity. It's not just about making beautiful and functional things; it's about making a powerful statement of self-belief. Your sewing projects are not mere creations; they are the manifestation of your artistic vision and the reflection of your evolving creativity. Through each stitch and every artistic choice, you'll discover that creativity is a boundless wellspring of self-empowerment, waiting to be unleashed in every project you undertake. It's an art that empowers you to embrace your unique perspective, to draw inspiration from the world, to experiment with new ideas, to embrace your shine, and to transform your creative dreams into realities. In the world of sewing, creativity becomes a dynamic force of self-expression and empowerment, an ever-evolving journey of artistic growth, and a beautiful testament to the power of self-belief.

Overcoming Self-Doubt

Self-doubt, that nagging voice of uncertainty, is a formidable adversary on the journey to self-empowerment. It lurks in the corners of our minds, questioning our abilities and challenging our self-worth. However, in the world of sewing, self-doubt can be confronted and overcome. This creative practice offers a unique platform to conquer self-doubt, fostering a sense of self-belief and empowerment.

Self-doubt often arises when we face new challenges or venture into uncharted territories. The creative world of sewing is no exception. It's a vast landscape with countless techniques, patterns, and possibilities, and it's natural to feel a sense of trepidation when you encounter a sewing project that's outside your comfort zone. Self-doubt whispers that you might not be skilled enough or experienced enough to tackle such endeavors. However, sewing provides a powerful antidote to this self-doubt. It reminds you that every skilled sewist was once a beginner, and every intricate stitch was once unfamiliar.

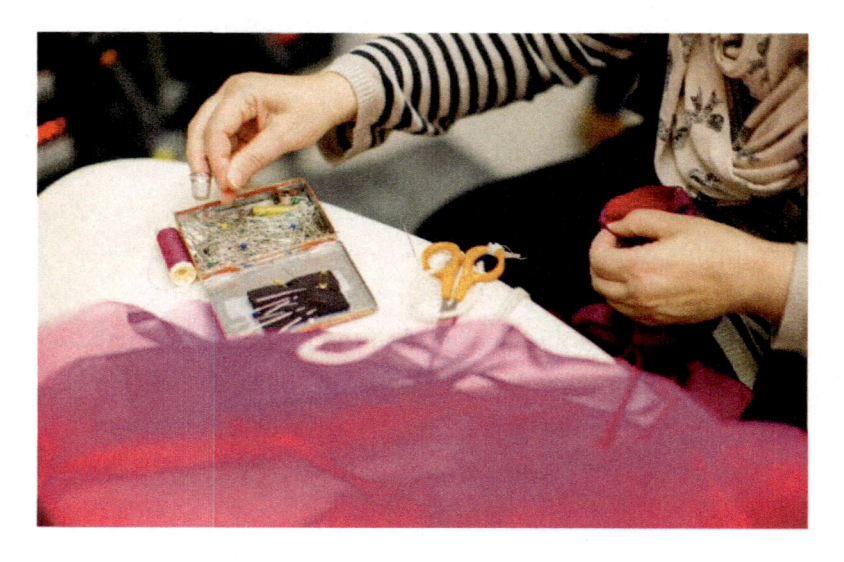

In the process of sewing, you begin to recognize that self-doubt is not a sign of inadequacy but a sign of growth. Each moment of doubt is an opportunity to learn and improve. The act of overcoming self-doubt becomes a testament to your inner strength. It signifies your capacity to confront challenges head-on and emerge victorious.

Moreover, sewing is a discipline that encourages experimentation. It invites you to step outside your comfort zone, try new techniques, and explore different styles. This experimental spirit is a powerful tool for confronting self-doubt. As you embark on uncharted sewing projects, you realize that the most remarkable growth occurs when you push beyond your perceived limits.

In these moments, self-doubt transforms into self-discovery. You unveil hidden talents, acquire new skills, and gain confidence in your creative abilities. This transformation is not limited to the sewing room but extends into all aspects of your life. It teaches you that self-doubt is not an insurmountable obstacle but a stepping stone to self-improvement.

Furthermore, sewing projects are tangible markers of your progress. When you complete a challenging project, whether it's a complex garment or an intricate quilt, you gain a sense of accomplishment. This sense of achievement is a powerful weapon against self-doubt. It reminds you that you are capable of conquering self-imposed limitations and that you have the tenacity to succeed in the face of adversity.

In sewing, every project is a reminder that self-doubt can be conquered. It becomes a catalyst for self-belief and personal empowerment. As you navigate the world of sewing, you discover that self-doubt is not a permanent companion but a transient visitor who can be shown the door. It teaches you that the path to self-empowerment is not devoid of self-doubt but is marked by your ability to confront and overcome it.

As you can see, sewing offers a unique opportunity to conquer self-doubt. It empowers you to step beyond your comfort zone, and gain a sense of accomplishment. It illustrates that self-doubt is not a measure of your capabilities but a challenge to be surmounted. In the creative world of sewing, you'll discover that self-doubt is not an adversary but a catalyst for growth and personal empowerment. It's a powerful reminder that you have the inner strength to face your doubts and emerge stronger on the other side.

Completing Beautiful Sewing Projects

Sewing is a journey of creativity and self-expression. It's a practice that takes you from envisioning a project to the satisfaction of a completed work of art. The joy of selecting fabrics, the careful consideration of patterns, and the meticulous stitching all culminate in the creation of beautiful sewing projects. This journey is a testament to your creative potential and a powerful tool for self-empowerment.

Sewing projects offer a unique canvas for your creativity. From crafting your wardrobe to designing home decor or making gifts for loved ones, each project is an opportunity to bring your unique vision to life. The process of selecting fabrics, patterns, and colors is an artistic endeavor in itself. It's a form of self-expression that mirrors your individuality and style.

The act of transforming fabric into a finished project is not just about creating something beautiful; it's about crafting a story. Each assignment carries with it the memories of selecting fabrics, the anticipation of starting, the dedication required to see it through, and the satisfaction of completion. These stories become a part of your creative journey, reminding you of your ability to transform ideas into tangible creations.

The satisfaction of completing a sewing project is a powerful antidote to self-doubt. It reaffirms your capability to set goals, persevere, and achieve them. In a world where self-doubt often lingers in the background, the act of completing a beautiful sewing project is a tangible reminder that you have the power to overcome challenges and fulfill your creative vision.

Moreover, sewing projects are tangible markers of your progress. As you tackle more complex projects and learn new techniques, you're not only adding to your skillset but also building self-confidence. The sense of accomplishment that comes with completing a challenging project boosts your self-esteem and empowers you to take on even more significant creative challenges.

Sewing is an art that celebrates imperfection. In the sewing room, there is no room for self-criticism, only room for self-expression. Each stitch may carry its unique character, and each project may have its quirks, but these just show your growth as a sewist. They teach you to embrace the beauty of imperfection, not just in your projects but also in yourself.

The act of completing a beautiful sewing project is an affirmation of your creativity and a source of immense pride. It serves as a tangible symbol of your ability to transform your ideas into reality. This sense of achievement extends beyond the sewing room and permeates all aspects of your life. It becomes a powerful tool for self-empowerment, reminding you that you can conquer challenges and create beauty in the world.

Completing beautiful sewing projects is not just about making practical or decorative items; it's about crafting stories, building self-confidence, and becoming the best version of yourself. It's a journey of self-expression that empowers you to set and achieve creative goals. Each project is proof of your creative potential and a reminder that you have the capacity to transform your ideas into beautiful, tangible creations. The completion of a sewing project is not just a finish line; it's a milestone on your journey to self-empowerment and creative fulfillment.

Celebrating Your Achievements

In the world of sewing, achievements come in many forms. From the completion of your first hand-sewn project to the intricate masterpiece that took months to finish, each step in your sewing journey is an achievement. However, often, in the hustle and bustle of life, these moments of accomplishment can be overlooked. It's crucial to pause, acknowledge, and celebrate your achievements in sewing, for they serve as a powerful source of self-empowerment and motivation.

Sewing is not merely a craft; it's a journey of personal growth and creative development. Every time you complete a project, you're not only producing a tangible item, but you're also showcasing your skills, determination, and artistic vision. The process of selecting fabrics, interpreting patterns, and bringing your project to life is a reflection of your creativity and commitment.

Every sewing project is a story in itself, composed of the moments of doubt, the decisions made, and the challenges conquered. When you reach the end of a project, you're not just finishing a piece of fabric; you're concluding a chapter in your creative narrative. Each project holds within it a piece of your journey, a record of your dedication, and a reflection of your artistic evolution.

Celebrating your achievements in sewing is not an act of vanity; it's a gesture of self-appreciation. It's a way to recognize your efforts and acknowledge your progress. Self-doubt often lurks in the background, questioning your abilities and undermining your self-worth. Celebrating your achievements is a powerful antidote to this doubt. It's a tangible reminder that you have the capability to overcome challenges, develop your skills, and complete what you set out to accomplish.

Moreover, celebrating your sewing achievements fosters self-confidence. As you acknowledge your successes, no matter how small or large, you build a sense of self-assurance. This self-confidence extends far beyond the sewing room. It becomes a part of your identity, reminding you that you have the capacity to set and achieve goals in all aspects of your life. It's a reminder that you can confront challenges and succeed.

In a world that often places immense emphasis on the final product, sewing teaches us to celebrate the process. Each step of a project, from selecting fabrics to stitching each seam, is a mini-victory. It's an opportunity to appreciate the journey, to take pride in the dedication and effort you've invested, and to recognize the joy of creation.

Every sewing achievement, regardless of its size or complexity, is a cause for celebration. Whether it's the first time you successfully create a straight seam or the moment you complete an intricate quilting project, each milestone represents personal growth and creative advancement. These achievements are not just markers on your sewing journey; they're symbols of your creative potential and your capacity for self-empowerment.

In conclusion, celebrating your achievements in sewing is not a mere act of self-congratulation; it's a vital aspect of personal growth and self-empowerment. It's a means to acknowledge your dedication, progress, and creativity. It's a reminder that you have the ability to set and achieve goals, both in sewing and in life. Every sewing achievement, no matter how small, is a step on your journey of self-empowerment and creative fulfillment.

Stitch 6: Rediscovering Joy in the Modern World

As we've already learned in the previous chapters, sewing is more than a craft; it's a practice that invites you to slow down, to embrace mindfulness, and to reconnect with your creative spirit. It offers an oasis of calm in the midst of the whirlwind of modern life.

Basically, it is an art that presents a unique path to rediscovering joy in this modern era.

This chapter delves into how sewing can be a vehicle for rekindling joy, fostering a sense of purpose, and enabling you to savor the beauty of the present moment.

In a world where we're often chasing the next achievement or the latest technology, sewing encourages you to pause and find contentment in the process itself. It's a journey of discovery that transcends the final product; it's about the stitches, the textures, and the creative journey. The act of sewing becomes a reminder that joy can be found in the act of creation, not just in the finished result. It's a practice that beckons you to rediscover the joy of crafting, embrace the simple pleasure of creativity, and celebrate the beauty of the present.

As we venture into this chapter, prepare to explore how sewing becomes a conduit to joy in our fast-paced, tech-savvy world. It's an art that not only produces beautiful, tangible creations but also rekindles the simple joy of making, of slowing down, and of cherishing the present.

The Impact of Technology and Fast Fashion

In the modern world, the pervasive influence of technology and the rise of fast fashion have significantly altered the way we engage with clothing, creativity, and the concept of self-expression. The implications of these changes are profound and are reflected in various aspects of our lives, from our personal identities to our environmental footprint.

The Technological Age and Clothing

The advent of technology has brought about a paradigm shift in the way we create, consume, and interact with fashion. It's not merely about the convenience of online shopping or the ubiquity of smartphones but the pervasive impact of technology on the fashion industry. From AI-powered design tools to digital fashion shows and virtual try-ons, technology is revolutionizing the fashion landscape.

1. **Online Shopping and E-Commerce:**

Online shopping has transformed the fashion industry. With the click of a button, consumers can access a global marketplace of clothing and accessories. It offers unparalleled convenience, a vast array of choices, and the ability to shop at any time. However, it also contributes to the disconnect between consumers and the physical act of sewing or creating garments.

2. **Fast Fashion:**

The rise of fast fashion retailers has led to an accelerated production cycle, with clothing collections changing at a rapid pace. This "throwaway culture" encourages consumers to buy more, discard more, and often undervalue the craftsmanship of clothing. It has become common for consumers to purchase garments with the expectation that they'll be worn only a few times before being discarded.

3. **Mass Customization and Personalization:**

Technology has also brought about a shift towards mass customization. While it allows consumers to have more control over their clothing choices, it often falls short of embracing the art of personal creation. Mass customization is a product of technology, not craftsmanship, which can lead to a loss of appreciation for the creative process of sewing.

Environmental Consequences

The surge in fast fashion, driven by technology, has profound environmental consequences. The demand for rapid production leads to overconsumption, increased waste, and a higher carbon footprint. The environmental impact of the fashion industry, from water usage to toxic chemicals in production, is a pressing global concern.

1. **Waste and Landfills:**

The fast fashion industry generates vast amounts of textile waste. The disposal of garments that have fallen out of favor contributes to overflowing landfills. The synthetic fibers in many fast fashion items take hundreds of years to decompose, adding to the problem.

2. **Resource Depletion:**

The production of textiles and clothing consumes immense amounts of resources, from water and energy to raw materials like cotton and oil-based synthetics. This places pressure on ecosystems and exacerbates resource scarcity.

3. **Chemical Pollution:**

The fast fashion industry's production processes often involve the extensive use of toxic chemicals. From dyeing fabrics to finishing treatments, these chemicals have far-reaching environmental impacts. Harmful substances leach into water sources and soil, leading to pollution and harm to ecosystems. Furthermore, the workers involved in the fashion supply chain, particularly in developing countries, may suffer adverse health effects due to exposure to these toxic chemicals.

4. **Microfiber Pollution:**

Fast fashion's reliance on synthetic materials, such as polyester and nylon, contributes to a lesser-known but significant issue: microfiber pollution. When these synthetic textiles are laundered, they shed tiny plastic microfibers that find their way into water bodies. These microfibers are challenging to filter and can accumulate in aquatic environments, posing risks to aquatic life and potentially entering the human food chain.

5. **Water Consumption:**

The fashion industry is a major consumer of water. From cotton cultivation to dyeing and finishing processes, water is a vital resource. However, this high water demand has dire consequences for water-scarce regions. The overuse of water contributes to the depletion of freshwater sources, disrupts local ecosystems, and exacerbates water scarcity issues in communities where water is a precious commodity.

6. **Carbon Footprint:**

The fast fashion model, characterized by rapid production cycles and transportation of goods over long distances, contributes significantly to greenhouse gas emissions. The carbon footprint of the fashion industry is substantial, with emissions resulting from manufacturing, transportation, and the disposal of clothing items. As consumers opt for frequent wardrobe turnover, the carbon footprint of fast fashion continues to grow.

7. **Ethical and Social Implications:**

The fast fashion industry's relentless pursuit of low-cost production has led to concerns about labor conditions, workers' rights, and ethical practices. In some cases, workers in the fashion supply chain face exploitation, unsafe working conditions, and inadequate wages. The drive to cut costs and meet demand at an ever-accelerating pace has consequences for the human rights of those involved in the industry.

8. **Consumer Behavior:**

Fast fashion relies on encouraging a culture of consumerism, where consumers are encouraged to continuously purchase new clothing items. This focus on rapid consumption can contribute to a throwaway culture, where clothing is discarded after minimal use, leading to excessive waste and further exacerbating the environmental impact.

As you can see, the environmental consequences of fast fashion driven by technology are far-reaching. They include overflowing landfills, resource depletion, chemical pollution, microfiber pollution, excessive water consumption, a substantial carbon footprint, ethical concerns, and a culture of consumerism. As we continue to explore the impact of technology and fast fashion on our modern world, it's essential to consider these environmental implications and to seek sustainable alternatives that align with a more environmentally conscious and ethical approach to fashion and creativity.

Sewing as a Counterbalance

In the face of the rapid changes brought about by technology and fast fashion, as well as its environmental consequences, sewing emerges as a powerful counterbalance. Sewing embodies values of sustainability, mindful consumption, and conscious creation that directly address the environmental challenges fast fashion perpetuates.

- **Sustainable Consumption:**

When you sew your clothing, you have control over the materials you use, allowing you to select eco-friendly and ethical options. This includes choosing fabrics made from sustainable sources, such as organic cotton, or upcycling materials from existing garments. By embracing these sustainable choices, you directly counteract the resource-intensive nature of fast fashion.

- **Reduction of Waste:**

Sewing encourages a reduction in textile waste. You can create garments tailored to your specific preferences and measurements, eliminating the need for purchasing multiple clothing items, many of which may end up in landfills. Moreover, sewing projects often utilize fabric remnants, minimizing waste in the process.

- **Appreciation for Craftsmanship and Durability:**

The act of sewing promotes craftsmanship and the creation of high-quality, long-lasting garments. Unlike fast fashion items, which are often designed with a limited lifespan, sewn garments are made to endure. This emphasis on durability reduces the need for frequent replacement, contributing to a more sustainable approach to fashion.

- **Mindful and Local Production:**

Sewing projects allow for the conscious production of clothing, often at a local level. This mindful approach to creation reduces the carbon footprint associated with the global transportation of fast fashion goods. By choosing to sew, you prioritize a smaller-scale, more sustainable mode of production.

- **Microfiber Awareness:**

Sewists are increasingly aware of the microfiber pollution issue associated with synthetic textiles. As such, they may choose natural and sustainable fabric options, thus contributing to reduced microfiber pollution.

- **Every Small Step Matters:**

Sewing embodies the principle that every small step towards sustainability matters. Whether it's using organic fabric, upcycling materials, or reimagining existing garments, each choice contributes to a more eco-conscious approach to clothing. These cumulative small steps, taken by sewing enthusiasts around the world, have the potential to make a significant impact in protecting the environment.

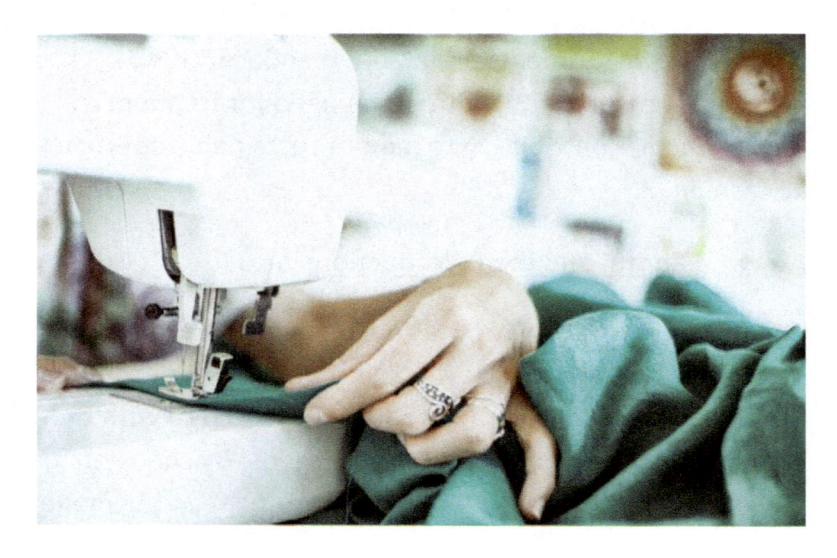

By embracing sewing as a counterbalance to fast fashion's environmental impact, individuals not only gain creative control over their wardrobes but also actively participate in reducing waste, promoting sustainability, and making choices that matter in the effort to protect the environment. In a world where every small step towards sustainability is significant, sewing emerges as a meaningful and empowering choice in the quest for a more eco-conscious approach to fashion and creativity.

Reconnecting with the Joy of Sewing
At its core, sewing embodies the essence of joy in creation. It rekindles the thrill that often gets buried under

the responsibilities of adulthood, akin to the unbridled pleasure of molding clay, painting, or building with blocks. The act of sewing reminds us that happiness doesn't reside solely in the possession of ready-made items but is found in the very process of crafting something with our own hands. The joy of sewing doesn't culminate in the finished product alone; it unfurls in the meticulous placement of each stitch, the choice of fabric, and the experience of getting lost in the creative flow.

But what sets sewing apart is its meditative nature. It demands focus and unwavering attention to detail. The repetitive rhythm of stitching can lead to a state of mindfulness, a tranquil space where the mind quiets and the cacophony of daily life recede into the background. It's a rare opportunity to be fully present in the moment, an oasis of serenity in a world defined by haste.

In the meditative process of sewing, individuals become attuned to the cadence of their breath, the gentle hum of the sewing machine, and the tactile sensations of fabric under their fingers. This mindfulness becomes a gateway to the joy that emanates from the act of creation. It reminds us that joy is not a destination but a journey, a journey found in the gentle inhales and exhales, in the repetitive but soothing nature of each stitch, and in the profound satisfaction of being wholly present.

At the same time, sewing acknowledges that joy lies not in the pursuit of perfection but in the continuous process of learning and growth. Mistakes are welcomed as opportunities to refine skills and add character to the final piece. Imperfection is not a hindrance but a source of uniqueness and charm.

Moreover, sewing reintroduces individuals to the sense of wonder that can wane with age. It rekindles the excitement of choosing colors, exploring textures, and envisioning the final outcome. It's a reminder that, in the simplest of things, wonder can be found. Sewing allows individuals to look at a stack of fabric or a basic pattern and see endless possibilities, reigniting their inner child's enthusiasm for exploration and creation.

Sewing is, above all, an avenue to rediscover joy and fulfillment. Completing a sewing project is not merely about having a new garment; it's about the profound satisfaction of having set a goal and achieved it. This sense of accomplishment is a wellspring of joy that reverberates into other spheres of life. It serves as a way to discover one's creative potential and the ability to set and attain goals.

In a world where joy can be elusive, fleeting, and sometimes even forgotten, sewing serves as a profound source of sustained joy. It offers a route to lasting happiness that's not dependent on ceaseless novelty but on the practice of creation and mindfulness. It reconnects individuals with the simple, unadulterated joy of sewing—a practice that offers a return to wonder, an embrace of mindfulness, and the profound fulfillment of creating something with one's own hands.

Flourishing Like Butterflies: Finding Happiness in Sewing

The craft of sewing is a transformative journey akin to the metamorphosis of a caterpillar into a butterfly. It's a process that unfolds with each stitch and every piece of fabric, offering individuals the opportunity to embrace happiness in its purest form. In the act of sewing, they discover the art of flourishing like butterflies—unfolding their wings to a world of creativity, fulfillment, and joy.

- **A Journey of Self-Discovery:**

The path of sewing is a profound journey of self-discovery. It's not merely about creating garments or accessories; it's about crafting a deeper connection with oneself. The process of selecting fabrics, choosing patterns, and bringing designs to life mirrors the process of self-discovery. It's an avenue for individuals to uncover their preferences, express their unique style, and, in doing so, unearth happiness.

Sewing allows individuals to curate their wardrobes in a way that resonates with their individuality. Each choice—whether it's the color of a fabric, the silhouette of a dress, or the finishing details—becomes a reflection of their inner selves. This process of self-expression is inherently joyful, as it enables them to manifest their personality and values in tangible, wearable forms.

- **Achievement and Creative Mastery:**

Happiness often lies in the sense of accomplishment. The journey of a sewing project—from the initial idea to the final stitch—offers numerous opportunities for achievement. It allows individuals to set goals, overcome challenges, and ultimately bring their creative visions to life. Each completed project becomes a manifestation of their creative mastery.

The joy of achieving something with their own hands is a profound one. It instills a sense of pride and self-worth, demonstrating that they are capable of creating and achieving. This sense of accomplishment can resonate throughout their lives, influencing how they approach other challenges and pursuits.

- **Flow and Mindfulness:**

Sewing is an immersive experience, a state of flow where time seems to stand still, and the outside world recedes into the background. The focused attention required in sewing demands mindfulness. It encourages individuals to be fully present in the moment, to lose themselves in the gentle rhythm of stitching and the tactile sensations of fabric under their fingers.

This state of mindfulness is a wellspring of happiness. It offers a respite from the constant noise and distractions of the modern world. In the act of sewing, individuals find solace, a serene space where they can tap into their creativity and inner calm. It's an escape from the demands of the external world, allowing them to rejuvenate their spirits and find genuine happiness in the process.

- **Nurturing a Sense of Community:**

Sewing is not just a solitary endeavor; it's also a means of connecting with a broader community. It fosters a sense of camaraderie with fellow sewing enthusiasts, offering opportunities to share ideas, techniques, and the joy of creation. In sewing circles, individuals often find a supportive and like-minded community.

This sense of belonging is a powerful source of happiness. It reminds individuals that they are not alone in their creative pursuits and that there are others who share their passions and who understand the joy that sewing brings. It bolsters their sense of connection and reminds them of the happiness that can be found in shared experiences.

The art of sewing is a transformative journey, a path to happiness that unfolds with every project. It's a journey of self-discovery, a voyage of creative mastery, and an immersion in mindfulness. It's a gateway to a sense of community, a reminder that happiness can be found not only in the creative act itself but in the connections formed along the way.

As individuals embark on this journey, they flourish like butterflies, spreading their wings to a world of creativity, fulfillment, and happiness. Sewing serves as a reminder that joy is not a distant destination but a path that can be traversed with every stitch and each moment spent in the creative process. It's an invitation to embrace the art of flourishing like butterflies, finding happiness in the beauty of self-expression and the serenity of creation.

Stitch 7: Teaching Students to Love Themselves

The concept of self-love holds immeasurable significance in our lives, especially in a world that is often marked by comparison and external standards. Teaching individuals, regardless of age, to embrace and nurture a profound love for themselves is an essential journey. It's a path that leads to a deeper sense of well-being, fulfillment, and resilience in the face of life's challenges. This chapter embarks on that very journey, exploring how the art of sewing becomes a remarkable vessel for imparting the invaluable lesson of self-love.

Sewing, beyond its practical and creative aspects, becomes a conduit for individuals to reacquaint themselves with self-compassion and self-esteem. It encourages them to see their worth, appreciate their unique qualities, and recognize their own beauty and strength. Through the act of sewing, they come to understand that the pursuit of self-love is not selfish but a fundamental necessity.

This chapter will delve into how sewing fosters self-love by providing a safe space for self-expression, allowing individuals to explore their way through the creative journey, and encouraging them to celebrate their achievements. It will explore how teaching students of all ages to love themselves through sewing can have profound and far-reaching effects, extending into various aspects of their lives.

The Importance of Self-Love and Self-Acceptance

In a world that constantly bombards us with images, ideals, and expectations,

The concepts of self-love and self-acceptance can often be confusing. With all the images, ideals, and expectations that we are bombarded with on a daily basis, it is easy to mistake self-love for selfishness. Even taking a moment for yourself can seem too much for a lot of people.

However, these qualities are not merely self-indulgent notions but are at the core of our well-being, mental health, and ability to navigate life's challenges with resilience and grace. The journey of self-love and self-acceptance is not a selfish trait; it is a fundamental necessity for a balanced and fulfilling life.

At its essence, self-love is the practice of treating ourselves with the same kindness, care, and compassion that we would offer to a dear friend. It's the art of extending love inward, nurturing our emotional and mental well-being, and embracing ourselves as we are. Self-acceptance, on the other hand, is the process of recognizing our own worth and acknowledging our strengths and weaknesses without judgment or criticism. It's an acknowledgment of our humanity and our unique qualities.

The importance of self-love and self-acceptance cannot be overstated. These qualities serve as the foundation for a healthy sense of self-worth and self-esteem. When we love and accept ourselves, we build a resilient core that can withstand the external pressures of societal expectations, peer comparisons, and the demands of a fast-paced world. We become better equipped to handle life's challenges, from setbacks and failures to stress and adversity.

Self-love and self-acceptance are not synonymous with complacency. They do not advocate for a lack of growth or self-improvement. Instead, they provide the emotional safety and inner strength needed to embark on a journey of personal development and self-actualization. When we love and accept ourselves, we are more open to learning, growth, and transformation. We become more willing to set goals, overcome obstacles, and strive for our aspirations, not out of a sense of inadequacy but out of a desire to reach our fullest potential.

Therefore, the importance of teaching self-love and self-acceptance cannot be understated. Young minds are impressionable, and the lessons they learn about themselves during their formative years can have a profound and lasting impact on their self-esteem and mental health. In an educational setting, self-love and self-acceptance are not only topics to be discussed but values to be instilled and practices to be cultivated.

Sewing as a vehicle for teaching self-love and self-acceptance is particularly powerful. It offers a space for individuals to express themselves. Through sewing, students learn that self-love is not tied to external measures of success or perfection but is a fundamental part of being human.

The importance of self-love and self-acceptance extends far beyond the individual. When individuals love and accept themselves, they become kinder, more compassionate, and more understanding of others. The ripples of self-love and self-acceptance extend into their relationships, their communities, and society as a whole. It fosters a world where individuals are not judged by their flaws but are celebrated for their uniqueness and their capacity for love.

With all the external pressures of the world that most people are perpetually dealing with, self-love and self-acceptance can serve as a beacon of light. It is a reminder that happiness, fulfillment, and mental well-being are not found in the pursuit of external standards but in the practice of loving and accepting oneself. It's a journey that unfolds with every act of self-compassion, with every acknowledgment of one's worth, and with every step taken towards becoming your best self.

Instilling Confidence Through Sewing

Confidence is a quality that can transform lives. It's the inner strength that allows individuals to face challenges, overcome obstacles, and believe in their own abilities. In today's world, instilling confidence is a vital component of empowering students to realize their full potential. Through the craft of sewing, the journey of self-confidence takes shape in a unique and transformative way.

Sewing provides a tangible platform for students to build and nurture their confidence. When they embark on a sewing project, they are venturing into the unknown, making choices, and creating something entirely unique. This act of creation instills a sense of self-belief as they see their designs take shape, one stitch at a time.

The process of sewing also teaches students the value of persistence. Sewing projects often come with their share of challenges, from threading needles to mastering intricate patterns. Overcoming these hurdles requires patience and resilience, skills that are transferrable to various aspects of life. As students persist in their sewing endeavors, they learn that it's okay to make mistakes and that perseverance can lead to success, enhancing their self-assurance.

Sewing is a practice that welcomes imperfection. It teaches students that perfection is not a requirement for self-worth or success. In the world of sewing, a crooked seam or an uneven hem is not seen as a failure but as an opportunity for growth and improvement. This approach encourages students to let go of the unrealistic pursuit of perfection that can stifle self-confidence in other areas of life.

Moreover, the act of sewing nurtures a sense of individuality. As students choose fabrics, patterns, and designs, they make creative decisions that reflect their unique tastes and preferences. This process helps them celebrate their individuality and develop confidence in their ability to make choices that align with their personal style. It fosters a belief in their capacity to express themselves authentically.

Sewing also encourages students to connect with a broader community of sewing enthusiasts. This sense of belonging and shared passion bolsters their self-confidence. This shared experience fosters a belief in their own abilities and reinforces their sense of self-worth.

In essence, sewing is not merely about crafting clothing and accessories; it's about crafting self-confidence. It provides students with a canvas for creative expression, a platform for learning persistence, and a community that supports and celebrates their individuality. Through sewing, students learn that self-confidence is not an abstract quality but a tangible and achievable one. It's a journey that unfolds with every stitch, fostering a belief in their creativity, resilience, and unique identity.

It's not just about creating beautiful things; it's also about creating a more confident you. Here are some tips to help you along the way:

- **Start Simple, Build Confidence:**

In the world of sewing, we begin with basic stitches and projects. It's like taking baby steps toward a more confident you. Each stitch you master is a stitch completing your canvas of self-assurance.

- **Unleash Your Creativity:**

Sewing allows you to make creative choices—choose fabrics, colors, and patterns that resonate with your unique style. This act of self-expression reinforces your self-belief.

- **Celebrate Small Achievements:**

Don't underestimate the power of celebrating even the tiniest milestones. Every hem stitched, every button sewn, show how much your skills are growing. These are the building blocks of your confidence.

- **Master Problem-Solving:**

Sewing often involves overcoming challenges. Whether it's a stubborn knot or a misaligned seam, consider them puzzles to solve. As you tackle each one, you sharpen your problem-solving skills and boost your confidence.

- **Embrace Mistakes as Lessons:**

Mistakes are not failures; they are stepping stones to growth. With each sewing error, you learn, adapt, and improve. These lessons are your secret allies in building confidence.

- **Constructive Feedback:**

Seek guidance and accept constructive feedback graciously. Remember, it's not about criticism; it's about refinement. Feedback helps you grow, and growth fuels confidence.

- **Collaborate and Shine:**

Collaborate with fellow sewers. Sharing ideas and learning from each other can be a confidence-enhancing experience. It's not just about creating; it's about the connections you make.

- **Break Goals into Achievable Steps:**

Like a seasoned seamstress, break down big sewing projects into smaller, manageable tasks. Completing these mini-goals fosters a sense of accomplishment and strengthens your self-belief.

- **Show Off Your Creations:**

Whether it's in a school showcase or simply sharing with friends and family, displaying your sewing creations is a powerful confidence boost. It's an affirmation of your creativity and your growing self-confidence.

- **Express Your Individuality:**

Your sewing projects are your canvas for self-expression. Every choice you make, from fabrics to design, reflects your unique style. Embrace your individuality; it's the heart of self-confidence.

- **A Supportive Environment:**

Remember, your sewing journey is in a supportive and judgment-free space. Mistakes are part of the creative process, and here, they're seen as opportunities to learn and grow.

- **Leverage Learning Resources:**

Books, online tutorials, and experienced sewers are your allies in this journey. They offer guidance, inspiration, and wisdom, helping you hone your sewing skills and build confidence.

- **Rise to Challenges:**

As you gain proficiency, take on more complex sewing projects. Each successful completion is a milestone that magnifies your self-confidence.

- **You Are Special:**

Embrace your uniqueness and your worth. Sewing is not just about crafting; it's about crafting a more confident, self-assured you. You are special, and you should be proud of yourself.

So, as you pick up your needle and thread, remember that each stitch is a step towards greater self-confidence. Sew, embrace, and believe in yourself - you've got this!

Stitch 8: A Workbook for Sewing and Well-being

Welcome to the last stage of your journey toward self-discovery, self-expression, and inner peace through the art of sewing. In this chapter, we will delve into the heart of the matter: how to create your personal workbook for sewing and well-being. This workbook will serve as your companion on this remarkable path, guiding you through the intricate stitches of self-awareness, creativity, and tranquility. Whether you're a seasoned seamstress or a novice, the power of sewing to nourish your mental and emotional well-being is available to all.

As we venture deeper into the world of sewing, we'll explore how to structure your workbook for maximum impact. We'll craft exercises and activities that promote mindfulness, self-reflection, and relaxation, intertwining the threads of creativity with the soothing rhythms of sewing. This chapter will provide you with the tools and insights needed to unlock the healing potential of this age-old craft.

Prepare to embark on a journey of self-discovery and well-being through the pages of your very own sewing workbook.

Interactive Sewing Exercises

While sewing as a craft is a great way to unwind, it can often be hard to find time for the practice. However, if you turn it into an activity, you may find it easier to complete your projects.

Here are a few ways you can turn sewing into an interactive exercise.

1. The Mindful Stitch

This exercise aims to encourage mindfulness and present-moment awareness while sewing. It will help you connect with your senses, focus on the task at hand, and embrace the therapeutic qualities of sewing.

Materials Needed:

1. Fabric scraps
2. Needle
3. Thread
4. Embroidery hoop (optional)
5. Scissors
6. A comfortable and quiet sewing space

Instructions

1. **Prepare Your Workspace:** Find a quiet, comfortable spot where you can concentrate without distractions. If you're using an embroidery hoop, secure your fabric in it to keep it taut. Thread your needle with a color of your choice, and tie a knot at the end of the thread.

2. **Take a Few Deep Breaths:** Before you begin, close your eyes and take a few deep breaths. Inhale slowly and gently through your nose, allowing your lungs to fill completely, and then exhale through your mouth. Let go of any tension or worries.

3. **Mindful Stitching:** With your eyes open, place the needle at the edge of your fabric. As you make your first stitch, focus all your attention on the physical sensations and details of the process:

- Notice the texture of the fabric against your fingertips.

- Feel the resistance as the needle passes through the fabric.

- Observe the sound of the thread sliding through the fabric.

- Pay attention to the colors and patterns on the fabric.

4. **Sew Slowly:** As you continue stitching, do it at a slow and deliberate pace. Each stitch is an

opportunity to practice mindfulness. Be fully present in each moment, letting go of any racing thoughts or distractions.

5. **Embrace Imperfection**: Allow yourself to make mistakes. If your stitches aren't perfectly even or straight, that's perfectly okay. This exercise is about the process, not the outcome. Imperfections are part of the beauty.

6. **Engage Your Senses:** Engage all your senses as you sew. This includes the gentle rustle of the fabric and the subtle scent of the thread. Immerse yourself in the tactile experience of each stitch.

7. **Breathe:** Don't forget to breathe! Continue taking slow, deep breaths as you sew. Let your breath anchor you in the present moment.

8. **Reflect on the Experience:** As you sew mindfully, take moments to reflect on the experience. What emotions, sensations, or thoughts arise? How does it feel to be fully present in this creative act?

9. **Create a Mindful Pattern:** Depending on your mood and the flow of your stitching, consider creating a mindful pattern. For example, you might deliberately make stitches in a meandering, interconnected pattern, like waves or a maze.

10. **End Mindfully:** When you feel satisfied with your mindful stitching exercise, end it mindfully as well.

Take a few deep breaths, acknowledge the tranquility you've cultivated, and express gratitude for this moment of creative mindfulness.

This practice can be repeated as often as you like, and the results need not be a finished project; it's about the process and the mindful journey. It's a way to infuse your sewing practice with a deeper sense of presence and serenity.

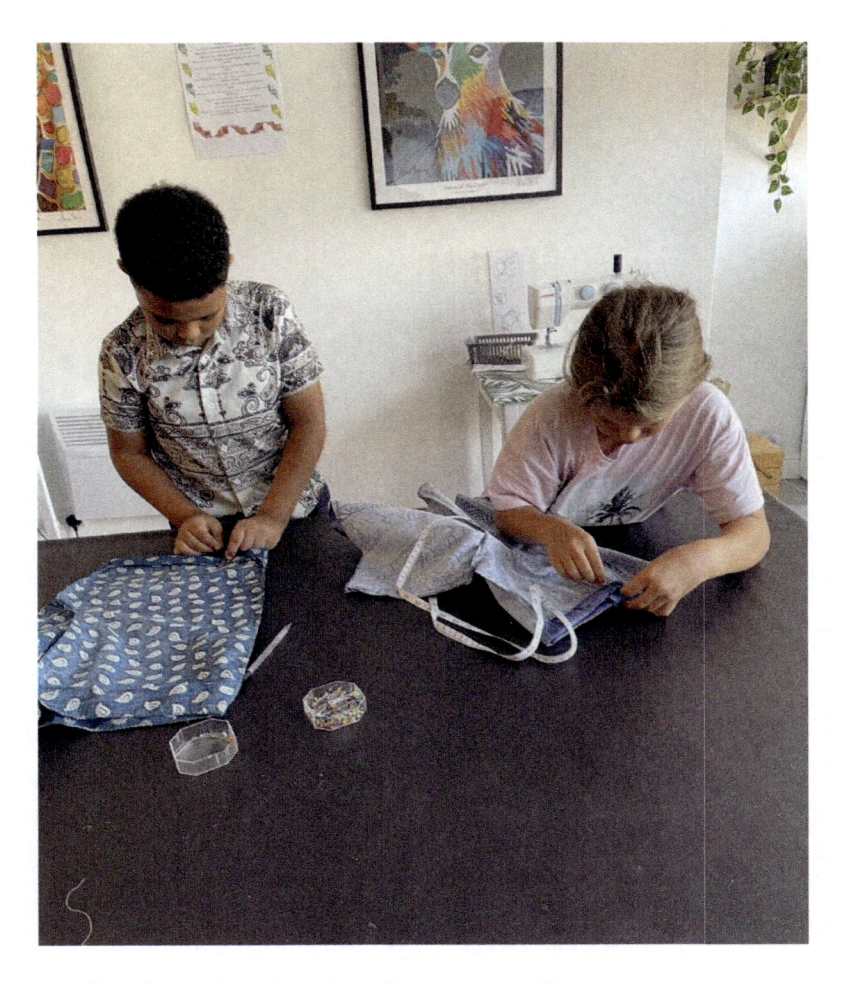

2. Creative Sewing Scavenger Hunt

This activity is designed to spark creativity, encourage exploration, and make sewing a fun adventure. It's perfect for children, beginners, or anyone looking to infuse excitement into their sewing projects.

Materials Needed:

1. Fabric scraps in various colors and textures

2. Needle

3. Thread

4. Scissors

5. Paper or sketchbook

6. Pencils

7. Sewing machine (optional)

8. A list of sewing prompts (explained below)

9. A sense of adventure

Instructions

1. **Prepare Your Sewing Materials:** Gather your sewing materials, including the fabric scraps, needles, thread, and scissors. If you're using a sewing machine, have it set up and ready to go.

2. **Create a Scavenger Hunt List:** Before you start sewing, create a list of sewing prompts or challenges. These prompts will guide your creative adventure. Examples of prompts include:

- Sew a zigzag pattern.

- Create a fabric flower.

- Make a mini quilt square.

- Sew a star shape.

- Craft a fabric animal.

3. **Choose Your Prompt**: Select a prompt from your list. This will be your sewing mission for this round. Feel free to choose prompts randomly or in a predetermined order.

4. **Find Fabric Treasures:** This is where the scavenger hunt part comes in! Explore your collection of fabric scraps and select pieces that match your chosen prompt. Let your imagination run wild as you search for the perfect fabrics.

5. **Plan Your Design:** Before you start sewing, plan your design. Sketch it out on a piece of paper if you like, or simply visualize it in your mind. What will your fabric creation look like?

6. **Sew Your Creation:** Once you have your design in mind and your fabric scraps ready, start sewing! Follow the prompt and use your selected fabrics to create your masterpiece. Whether you're hand sewing or using a machine, focus on bringing your vision to life.

7. **Embrace Creativity:** Don't be afraid to experiment and get creative. Use different stitches, combine fabrics, and let your imagination guide you. Remember, this is all about fun and exploration.

8. **Reflect and Repeat:** After completing your sewing creation, take a moment to reflect on what you've made. How did it turn out? What did you enjoy about the process? Then, pick another prompt from your list and start a new sewing adventure.

9. **Share Your Creations**: If you're doing this activity with others, gather to share and admire each other's creations. Discuss what inspired you and what you learned from each sewing adventure.

10. **Optional: Time-Based Challenge:** To add an extra layer of excitement, consider setting a timer for each prompt. Can you complete the sewing challenge within a specific time frame? It's like a sewing race!

This creative sewing scavenger hunt is a delightful way to infuse joy and exploration into your sewing projects. It encourages you to think outside the box, experiment with different techniques, and enjoy the process of sewing as an adventure. Have fun, get crafty, and let your imagination lead the way!

3. Collaborative Sewing Challenge

Sometimes, you need some company while taking on your next sewing endeavor. Not only is it a great team activity, but it also makes the entire process more fun and productive. This group sewing activity fosters teamwork, creativity, and a sense of shared accomplishment. It's perfect for sewing circles, workshops, or gatherings where participants can work together on a common project.

Materials Needed:

1. A large piece of fabric (size depends on the number of participants)
2. Sewing supplies (needles, thread, scissors)
3. Fabric scraps, buttons, beads, ribbons, and other embellishments
4. Sewing machine (optional)
5. A spacious work area

Instructions

1. **Prepare Your Workspace:** Ensure you have enough space for all participants to work comfortably. Lay out the large piece of fabric on tables or the floor.
2. **Choose a Theme:** Select a theme or concept for your collaborative sewing project. The theme could be as simple as "Nature," "Community," "Seasons," or something unique to your group's interests.
3. **Designate Zones:** If you have a large group, divide the fabric into sections, each assigned to a pair or group of participants. Each group will work on a different aspect of the project but within the same theme.

4. **Select Materials:** Set up a table with various fabric scraps, buttons, beads, ribbons, and other embellishments that fit the theme. Participants can choose materials to incorporate into their section of the collaborative project.

5. **Plan and Create:** Give participants some time to brainstorm and plan their contribution to the project. They can sketch their ideas on paper or discuss them with their group members. Then, let the sewing begin! Each group works on their designated section, sewing and embellishing as they go.

6. **Coordinate and Communicate:** Encourage participants to communicate with others working on adjacent sections of the fabric. This coordination ensures that the project flows seamlessly and that the different sections connect cohesively.

7. **Embrace Creativity:** Encourage participants to get creative with their designs. They can incorporate elements like appliqué, embroidery, quilting, or other sewing techniques to enhance their section of the project.

8. **Rotate and Collaborate:** At specific intervals or when each group feels they've completed their section, rotate the fabric to the next group. This

ensures that every participant has the opportunity to contribute to different parts of the project.

9. **Review and Refine:** Periodically step back as a group to review the collaborative project's progress. Discuss what's working well and make refinements as needed to maintain the overall theme and aesthetic.

10. **Finishing Touches:** Once all sections are completed, bring the project together as a whole. Add any final touches or embellishments to unify the different sections. If desired, stitch the sections together to create a finished piece.

11. **Display and Celebrate:** Display the completed collaborative project in your sewing space, community center, or event venue. Celebrate your collective creativity and teamwork with a group gathering or showcase.

This collaborative sewing challenge not only creates a beautiful piece of art but also strengthens the bonds within your group. It's a great way to encourage teamwork, celebrate individual creativity, and create a shared masterpiece that reflects the spirit of your sewing community.

4. Sewing Relay Race

Instead of working on a collaborative project together, this group activity encourages the participants to embrace their competitive spirit. The Sewing Relay Race is a fast-paced and exciting sewing competition that challenges participants' sewing skills, teamwork, and time management.

Materials Needed:

1. Sewing machines (one per team)
2. Fabric scraps
3. Thread
4. Scissors
5. Pins
6. Measuring tape
7. Seam rippers (for corrections)
8. A stopwatch or timer

Instructions

1. **Organize Teams:** Divide your participants into teams of equal size. Each team should have its own sewing machine, materials, and sewing station. The more teams there are, the more competitive and fun the relay will be.
2. **Set Up Stations:** Prepare a sewing station for each team, including a sewing machine, fabric scraps,

thread, pins, measuring tape, and scissors. Make sure each station is identical.

3. **Choose a Pattern:** Select a simple sewing pattern or project that each team will complete. It could be a basic tote bag, a pillowcase, or a small apron. Ensure that all teams have the same pattern to work on.

4. **Explain the Rules:** Clarify the rules to all participants. Each team member will have a specific role in the relay:

- Cutter: Responsible for cutting the fabric according to the pattern.

- Pinner: Pins the fabric pieces together.

- Sewer: Operates the sewing machine and stitches the pieces together.

- Quality Checker: Inspect the completed section for accuracy.

5. **Start the Relay:** When you say "go," the relay begins. The Cutter starts by cutting the fabric pieces, then passes them to the Pinner, who pins the pieces together. The Pinner then passes the pinned fabric to the Sewer, who uses the sewing machine to stitch the pieces together. Finally, the Sewer passes the partially completed project to the

Quality Checker, who inspects it for quality and accuracy.

6. **Handoffs and Transitions:** To ensure a smooth transition between roles, participants can use a designated area for handoffs. Teams should strategize and communicate to optimize their efficiency.

7. **Time the Relay:** Use a stopwatch or timer to track each team's completion time. The team that finishes the sewing relay first, with the most accurate and well-sewn project, wins the competition.

8. **Prizes and Recognition:** Celebrate the winning team with prizes or recognition. You can also acknowledge individual team members for their specific roles, such as "Fastest Cutter" or "Most Accurate Sewer."

9. **Repeat or Challenge:** To add more competition and excitement, you can have multiple rounds of the relay or introduce challenges, like sewing blindfolded for an extra layer of fun and complexity.

10. **Reflect and Improve:** After the relay, discuss what worked well and where improvements could be made. It's an opportunity to learn from the competition and enhance your sewing skills.

The Sewing Relay Race injects a dose of competitive energy into your sewing group or workshop. It's a fantastic way to test your sewing skills under time pressure, encourage teamwork, and have a blast while sewing.

Goal Setting for Your Creative Path

When embarking on a creative journey, goal setting can be a powerful tool. It helps you navigate your sewing projects, stay inspired, and measure your progress along the way.

Here are some tips on how to start.

Define Your Creative Vision

The first step in setting goals for your sewing projects is to define your creative vision. What inspires you? What do you want to achieve with your sewing skills? Are you drawn to fashion design, home décor, quilting, or crafting unique gifts? Understanding your creative vision helps you determine the direction your sewing goals will take.

Set Specific and Realistic Goals

Once you've established your creative vision, break it down into specific and realistic goals. Specific goals are clear and well-defined, while realistic goals are attainable within your skill level, resources, and timeframe. For example, if your vision is to create a handmade wardrobe, a specific goal could be to sew a pair of pants or a dress by a certain date.

Prioritize Your Goals
Not all sewing goals are of equal importance. Prioritize your goals by considering which projects are most meaningful to you and which align with your creative vision. This ensures that you're working on the projects that inspire and fulfill you the most.

Set Measurable Milestones
To track your progress and stay motivated, set measurable milestones for each goal. These milestones act as checkpoints along your creative path. For instance, if your goal is to complete a quilt, a measurable milestone could be finishing the quilt top and then quilting and binding it.

Timeframe and Deadlines
Assign a timeframe or deadline to each goal and milestone. A timeline creates a sense of urgency and helps you manage your time efficiently. However, be realistic with your deadlines to prevent feeling overwhelmed.

Stay Adaptable
Life is unpredictable, and sometimes, unexpected events may impact your sewing goals. Stay adaptable and be open to adjusting your goals and deadlines when necessary. Flexibility is key to maintaining a positive sewing experience.

Reflect and Celebrate Achievements
Regularly reflect on your progress and celebrate your achievements, no matter how small. Acknowledging your successes keeps you motivated and reinforces your commitment to your creative path.

Seek Support and Accountability
Sharing your sewing goals with friends, sewing groups, or online communities can provide valuable support and accountability. They can offer guidance, encouragement, and constructive feedback to help you achieve your goals.

Remember that your creative path is a personal journey, and there's no one-size-fits-all approach to goal setting. Tailor your goals to suit your individual interests and aspirations. Whether you're sewing for relaxation, self-expression, or to master a new skill, setting goals will enrich your sewing experience and lead you to meaningful accomplishments.

Create Your Personal Sewing Workbook

Here are some actionable tips for goal setting and how to start creating your own personal sewing workbook.

- **Start with Clear Intentions:**

Begin by defining your creative intentions and what motivates you to sew. Is it the joy of crafting unique garments, creating thoughtful gifts, or simply honing your sewing skills? Your intentions will guide your goal setting.

- **Create a Sewing Journal:**

Maintain a sewing journal or a digital note-taking app to record your goals, ideas, and progress. This journal serves as a valuable reference point and a place to jot down new projects as they come to mind.

- **Set SMART Goals:**

Use the SMART criteria to structure your goals:

- Specific: Clearly define what you want to achieve.
- Measurable: Include specific criteria to track your progress.
- Achievable: Ensure that your goal is within reach and realistic.

- Relevant: Align your goal with your creative vision and interests.

- Time-bound: Set a deadline to create a sense of urgency.

- **Break Down Larger Goals:**

If you have ambitious sewing projects in mind, break them down into smaller, manageable tasks and milestones. This prevents feeling overwhelmed and keeps you focused.

- **Create a Priority List:**

Prioritize your sewing projects and goals based on your level of enthusiasm, the season, or any upcoming events. This helps you decide where to allocate your time and resources.

- **Plan a Weekly Sewing Schedule:**

Dedicate specific days or times during the week for sewing. A structured schedule ensures you consistently work toward your goals.

- **Regularly Review Your Goals:**

Set aside time monthly or quarterly to review your goals and progress. Reflect on what you've accomplished, adjust your goals as needed, and celebrate your achievements.

- **Set Up a Dedicated Sewing Space:**

Having a well-organized and clutter-free sewing space can increase productivity and motivation. Ensure your tools and materials are easily accessible.

- **Learn and Improve Skills:**

Include skill-based goals in your sewing journey. Whether it's mastering a new stitch or conquering a particular sewing technique, expanding your skill set can be rewarding.

- **Experiment and Take Risks:**

Don't be afraid to try new things. Experiment with different fabrics, patterns, and designs. Taking risks in your projects can lead to unexpected creative breakthroughs.

- **Seek Inspiration:**

Stay inspired by following sewing blogs and social media accounts or attending sewing exhibitions and workshops. Exposure to new ideas can fuel your creativity.

Personal Sewing Journey Workbook

This workbook is your companion on your creative sewing adventure. Use it to set goals, reflect on your progress, and grow as a skilled seamstress.

Let's get started!

How to Use This Workbook

- Take your time to complete each section.
- Be honest and open with yourself.
- Celebrate your achievements along the way.

Section 1: Discover Your Sewing Style

Sewing Preferences

- What types of sewing projects do you enjoy the most?
- Are you drawn to classic or contemporary styles?

Color Palette

- List your favorite colors for sewing projects.
- Experiment with color combinations you'd like to try.

Inspiration Board

- Collect images, fabric swatches, and patterns that inspire you.
- Create a visual representation of your sewing vision.

Section 2: Setting Sewing Goals
Short-Term Goals

- List two to three sewing goals for the next month.
- Be specific about what you want to achieve.

Long-Term Goals

- Envision where you want to be in a year.
- Set ambitious yet realistic goals to work toward.

Goal Tracking

- Use the chart below to track your progress.
- Celebrate each goal you accomplish!

Sewing Goals Tracker

- Here is a sample goal tracker that you can use to track your progress.

Goal	Deadline	Progress	Completed

Goal 1

Goal 2

Goal 3

Goal 4

Goal 5

Section 3: Sewing Project Planner
Project Ideas

- Brainstorm ideas for future sewing projects.

- Include garments, accessories, or home decor items.

Project Details

- Choose a project and list the materials needed.

- Estimate the time it will take to complete.

- Assess the level of difficulty.

Budget Tracker

- Stay within your budget by recording expenses for each project.

- Be mindful of your sewing-related spending.

Section 4: Skill Development
Technique Log

- List sewing techniques you've mastered or want to learn.

- Note where you can find resources to improve your skills.

Skill Building Exercises

- Practice essential stitches, seams, and patterns.

- Challenge yourself to tackle new techniques.

Feedback and Improvement

- Reflect on your completed projects.

- Write down what went well and areas for growth.

Section 5: Personal Sewing Journal
Daily/Monthly Entries

- Write about your daily sewing activities.

- Share your challenges, triumphs, and discoveries.

Mood Tracker

- Record your mood before and after sewing sessions.

- Observe how sewing affects your emotional well-being.

Gratitude Corner

- Express gratitude for the joy sewing brings to your life.
- Acknowledge the skills you've gained through sewing.

Section 6: Community Engagement
Sewing Circle

- Share your experiences from sewing meet-ups or online communities.
- Discuss the insights you've gained through collaboration.

Collaborative Projects

- Detail any group projects you've participated in.
- Explain the skills you contributed and what you learned.

Section 7: Resources and Recommendations
Favorite Sewing Blogs/Channels

- List blogs, YouTube channels, or social media accounts that inspire you.

- Include brief notes on why you find them valuable.

Recommended Tools

- Note your favorite sewing tools and equipment.
- Include brands and specifications for reference.

Book and Pattern Reviews

- Share your thoughts on sewing books and patterns you've tried.
- Mention what you liked and any areas for improvement.

Section 8: Personal Sewing Challenges
Monthly Challenges

- Participate in sewing challenges and document your entries.
- Share your experiences and the lessons learned.

Create Your Challenge

- Design your sewing challenge tailored to your interests.
- Set your own rules and see how it motivates you.

Section 9: Reflection and Growth
Reflection Questions

- Answer prompts about your sewing journey, challenges, and goals.

- Use this space to express your thoughts and ambitions.

Document Your Progress:

- Take photos of your completed projects and share them with friends and family.

- Seeing how far you've come can be incredibly motivating.

Visual Progress Board

- Create a visual representation of your sewing journey.

- Showcase your completed projects and acquired skills.

Conclusion

Congratulations on completing your Personal Sewing Journey Workbook! Remember that every stitch you make is a step forward in your creative sewing adventure. Keep sewing, setting goals, and celebrating your achievements. Your journey is unique, and your growth is inspiring. Enjoy every moment of it!

Next Steps

- Continue to set and achieve your sewing goals.

Tracking Your Mental and Emotional Well-being

Part of the reason why we started this sewing journey was to fight your stress away. Therefore, it is crucial that you also keep a check on your mental and emotional well-being while you continue your sewing journey.

Start a Well-being Journal:

Begin by maintaining a journal where you can record your thoughts and emotions regularly. This journal serves as a safe space to express your feelings and assess your mental and emotional health over time.

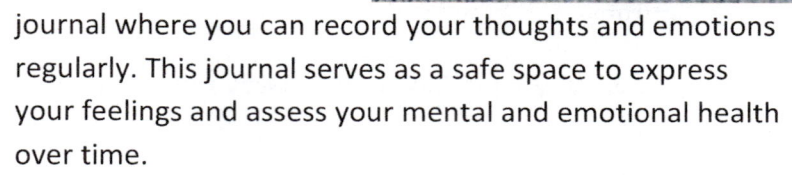

Daily Reflection:

Dedicate a few minutes each day to reflect on your feelings. Ask yourself questions like:

- How do I feel today?
- What events or situations affected my mood?
- Did I experience stress or anxiety today?

- What made me feel happy or fulfilled?

Mood Tracking:

Use a mood-tracking app or create a simple chart to monitor your daily moods. Assign a color or label to each mood (e.g., happy, sad, anxious) and mark your mood for the day.

Emotional Awareness:

Pay attention to your emotional responses during the day. Recognize patterns in your emotional reactions to specific events or triggers. This awareness can help you identify areas that may need attention.

Stress and Anxiety Logs:

Maintain logs for stress and anxiety triggers. Note what situations or circumstances tend to cause stress or anxiety, and identify strategies to manage these challenges.

Self-Care Routine:

Track your self-care routine. Include activities that promote mental and emotional well-being, such as meditation, exercise, reading, or creative pursuits. Assess how regularly you engage in these activities.

Sleep Quality:

Keep a sleep journal to monitor your sleep patterns. Track the duration of sleep, quality of sleep, and any disruptions. Adequate rest is crucial for emotional health.

Gratitude Journal:

Include a gratitude journal as part of your well-being tracking. Write down things you're thankful for each day. Focusing on gratitude can boost your overall mood.

Monthly and Yearly Assessments:

Periodically review your journal entries, mood charts, and emotional logs. Assess how your mental and emotional well-being has evolved over time. This long-term perspective can reveal significant insights.

Create a Supportive Network:

Maintain connections with friends and loved ones who can provide emotional support. Reach out to them when you need to talk or share your feelings. Make sure to also be there for them when they are in need of emotional support to create a healthy and long-lasting bond.

Adjust Your Approach:

Use the insights gained from tracking to adjust your approach to self-care and well-being. If certain activities consistently uplift your mood, prioritize them in your routine. If you identify triggers of stress or anxiety, work on coping strategies.

Stay Mindful:

Practice mindfulness techniques to stay present and aware of your emotions. Mindfulness can help you manage stress and improve your emotional responses.

Seek Professional Help:

If you notice persistent negative changes in your mental and emotional well-being, consider seeking professional help from a therapist, counselor, or psychologist. They are better qualified to provide proper guidance and support.

Reflecting on Your Sewing Journey

Sewing, a craft often seen as the simple act of stitching fabric, holds a deeper meaning. Beyond the garments produced, it weaves a journey of creativity and personal growth.

Every sewing journey commences with the first few stitches, much like stepping into the unknown. As you select fabrics, choose patterns, and guide the needle, you are entering a world that requires learning, patience, and practice. These early stages teach you valuable life lessons:

persistence, patience, and the value of gradual progress.

Each sewing project you complete is a self-portrait painted with fabric and thread. Your choices of patterns, colors, and styles are reflections of your identity and evolving tastes. The garments you create are more than just clothes; they are expressions of your creativity and personal style.

In the process of crafting, you encounter both successes and challenges. Patterns that initially seemed complex become achievable with persistence. Seams that once caused frustration now lay flat and straight. Mistakes turn into lessons, and setbacks become stepping stones for future endeavors.

One of the most remarkable aspects of sewing is the resilience it imparts. Every project is a journey in itself, with its unique twists and turns. You face sewing mishaps, broken needles, and fabrics that resist your efforts, yet you persist. This resilience translates to life's challenges as well. You learn to adapt, problem-solve, and forge ahead when life throws curveballs.

And while the pursuit of perfection is a noble goal, you discover that the minor imperfections add character and uniqueness to your creations. Imperfections are not flaws; they are opportunities for growth and learning.

Completing a sewing project is a moment of triumph. The satisfaction of finishing a project reminds you of the joy that results from effort and dedication. It is a tangible representation of your ability to set a goal, work toward it, and achieve it. In a world marked by constant change, sewing provides a sanctuary of consistency. The steady hum of the sewing machine, the rhythmic motion of the needle, and the gradual transformation of fabric into a finished piece serve as anchors in a rapidly shifting world.

As you continue sewing, your journey unfolds with new patterns, fabrics, and experiences. Your skills evolve, and your confidence grows. The sewing journey is not just about creating beautiful garments; it's about crafting a beautiful life. It's a journey that teaches you patience, resilience, self-acceptance, and the value of progress. It's a journey that weaves together threads of creativity, personal growth, and self-discovery into a tapestry uniquely yours.

In retrospect, your sewing journey is a testament to your growth and the beauty of the ongoing journey. It's a journey that promises countless more stitches, challenges, and moments of pure creative joy.

Conclusion

In our journey through the world of sewing, we've ventured from selecting fabrics and threading needles to uncovering the therapeutic and creative dimensions of this craft. It's been a hands-on exploration, as we've learned the basics and delved into how sewing can positively impact our well-being.

But what's next? How do we connect the practical aspects of sewing to our daily lives? How do we take the skills we've acquired and apply them beyond the sewing room?

This journey is more than a mere pastime; it's a guide for self-improvement. The patience you've developed while wrestling with intricate patterns is for more than just sewing projects. It's a valuable life skill that helps you navigate real-world challenges. The perseverance you've demonstrated when redoing crooked seams can be adapted to solve life's complex problems.

Your sewing space isn't just a creative retreat; it's a place to find serenity and consistency amidst life's chaos. The contentment you experience when completing sewing projects reflects the satisfaction of achieving your life's goals step by step.

As we conclude this book, let's explore how the practical lessons you've learned from your sewing journey can harmonize with your daily life. It's about discovering how your sewing skills and experiences are transferrable and applicable to the everyday challenges and goals you face.

Your sewing journey isn't just a single thread; it's woven into the fabric of your life. And even though this book is concluding, your sewing journey is a continuous adventure, ready to embrace new opportunities and continued growth.

The Endless Possibilities of Sewing for Well-being

As we wrap up this book, it's crucial to emphasize the endless possibilities that sewing offers for your overall well-being. Sewing isn't just a one-size-fits-all craft; it's adaptable to your unique needs and preferences.

Here's a glimpse of how sewing can enrich your life in a myriad of ways:

- Stress Relief: The rhythmic and repetitive nature of sewing can soothe your nerves, making it an effective stress relief tool. Whether you're quilting, embroidering, or simply stitching by hand, the act of sewing can serve as a form of meditation, helping you find tranquility in the midst of a hectic world.

- Therapeutic Expression: Use sewing as a means of self-expression. Your choice of fabrics, colors, and designs can reflect your personality and emotions.

Creating something beautiful can be a powerful form of self-therapy and a way to channel your feelings constructively.

- <u>Social Connection:</u> Sewing can be a fantastic way to connect with others who share your passion. Joining a sewing group or participating in workshops can lead to new friendships, fostering a sense of community that enhances your overall well-being.

- Skill Development: The learning curve in sewing is a journey of its own. Continually improving your skills and tackling more complex projects can boost your self-esteem and sense of accomplishment. Each new skill acquired is a small victory that adds to your self-confidence.

- Personalized Self-Care: Sewing is not just about creating beautiful garments; it's about making time for yourself. Designate your sewing time as a form of self-care, a moment to step back from daily stresses and indulge in a creative pursuit that nurtures your spirit.

- Emotional Release: Like squeezing a stress ball, the physicality of sewing can help release pent-up emotions. The satisfaction of completing a project is like a mini celebration, providing a positive emotional boost.

- Sense of Purpose: The act of sewing can give you a sense of purpose. Whether you're sewing for yourself, your family, or for a charitable cause, knowing that your work has a tangible impact on others can be deeply fulfilling.

- Mindful Living: Sewing encourages mindfulness. It demands your attention and presence, allowing you to let go of worries about the past or future. In this sense, it can be a gateway to a more mindful, grounded way of life.

- Creative Exploration: The possibilities within sewing are virtually limitless. From clothing and home decor to quilting and crafting, you have a vast array of creative avenues to explore. This creative freedom can spark joy and passion, essential elements of overall well-being.

As you continue your sewing journey, keep in mind that there's no one right way to sew for well-being. Your path is uniquely yours, and the possibilities are endless. Whether you find solace in the soothing rhythm of the sewing machine or delight in the intricate details of hand embroidery, sewing has something to offer everyone.

So, embrace the potential for positive change that sewing brings and let it enrich your life in ways you never imagined.

A Call to Action: Spread the Joy of Sewing

As you've journeyed through the art and science of sewing for well-being, you've likely discovered the transformative power this craft holds. The final pages of this book serve as a call to action—an invitation to share the joy of sewing with others and extend the benefits you've experienced. Here are some ways to do just that:

- Teach and Inspire: If you've developed sewing skills and a passion for the craft, consider teaching others. Host workshops, classes, or online tutorials to help beginners embark on their own sewing journey. Sharing your knowledge not only benefits others but also deepens your understanding and appreciation of sewing.

- Mentorship: Offer mentorship to individuals, especially younger generations, who may not have had the opportunity to learn the art of sewing. Pass on your skills and encourage them to explore their creativity and cultivate resilience.

- Community Projects: Collaborate with local communities to undertake sewing projects for a cause. Create blankets for shelters, sew masks during health crises, or craft clothing for those in need. These projects not only provide valuable items but also strengthen the sense of community and shared purpose.

- Empower through Creativity: Encourage those around you to use sewing as a tool for empowerment. Emphasize that the process is more important than the outcome. Remind them that it's okay to embrace imperfections and view mistakes as stepping stones to success.

- Share Your Story: Your sewing journey is a unique story worth sharing. Blog about your experiences, post on social media, or write articles for local publications. Your narrative can inspire others to pick up a needle and thread, fostering a broader community of sewing enthusiasts.

- Create a Sewing Club: Form a sewing club or join an existing one. These clubs serve as spaces for shared learning, camaraderie, and creative exploration. They are excellent platforms for expanding the joy of sewing to a wider audience.

- Gift Handcrafted Creations: The act of gifting handmade items is a powerful way to introduce others to the world of sewing. Handcrafted gifts are not just physical tokens of affection; they represent the care, effort, and love put into their creation.

- Foster Self-Love: Sewing isn't just about creating tangible objects; it's about nurturing self-love. Encourage individuals to embark on their sewing journey as a form of self-care. It's an opportunity for them to slow down, find peace, and gain a sense of accomplishment.

By taking action and sharing the joy of sewing, you extend the benefits of this craft far beyond your personal experience. You become a part of a movement that fosters creativity, resilience, and emotional well-being. In the process, you weave stronger bonds with your community and leave a legacy of positivity and empowerment for generations to come.

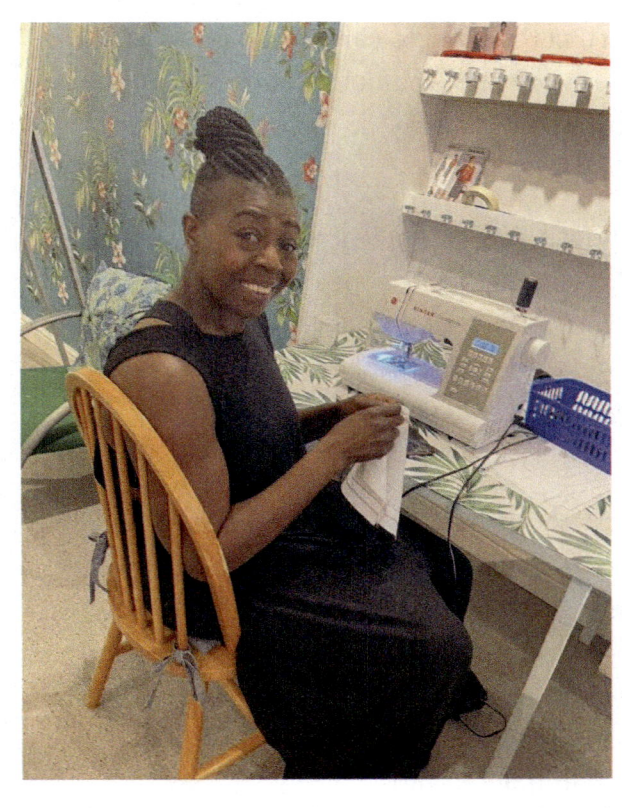

As you close this book and embark on your own journey of spreading the joy of sewing, remember that it's the simple act of extending a helping hand, teaching a new skill, or sharing your passion that can spark profound change in the lives of others.

Your Sewing and Well-being Journey Ahead

As we near the end of this book, I want to take a moment to reflect on the path we've walked together, exploring the art and science of sewing for well-being. It has been a remarkable journey of creativity, self-discovery, and empowerment, and I'm genuinely grateful that you've joined me on this journey.

Now, as you turn the page to close this chapter, I want to offer a few parting thoughts to carry with you as you continue your sewing and well-being journey. Your adventure doesn't conclude here; in fact, it's just beginning.

Remember, the stitches you've learned, the projects you've completed, and the inner peace you've discovered are all valuable tools in your daily life. The skills you've honed, like patience, problem-solving, and resilience, aren't limited to the sewing room. They can be applied to any challenge life presents.

Sewing isn't just about creating beautiful garments or exquisite quilts; it's a form of self-expression. It's a way to bring your inner world to life through fabrics and threads. Don't hesitate to use this form of creativity to convey your thoughts and emotions. Whether through the clothes you wear or the gifts you craft, let your creations be an expression of your unique spirit.

Sewing is not just a solitary act; it's a bridge to others who share your passion. Seek out sewing communities, join workshops, and connect with kindred spirits. The joy of sewing is often multiplied when shared with others, and you'll find inspiration in the diverse perspectives of fellow enthusiasts.

As you sew, let your projects be a reflection of your personal journey. Celebrate your successes and learn from your mistakes. Each project, no matter how simple or complex, is a testament to your growth and creativity. Your sewing room is a space where self-acceptance is encouraged and that is what makes your creations truly yours.

And just like that, you've become a part of the big family at Artisan Sewing School, including these happy and content students with their projects:

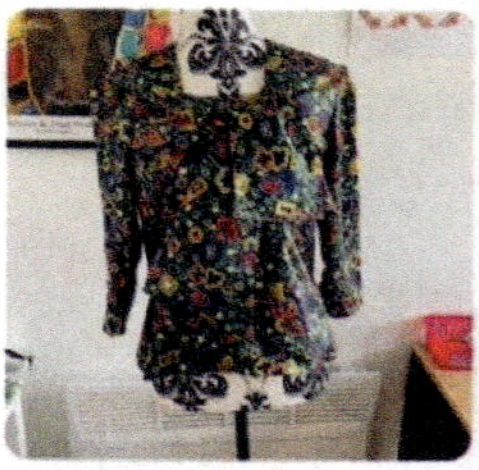
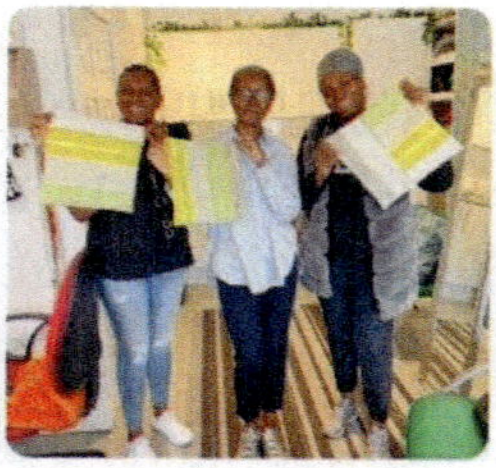
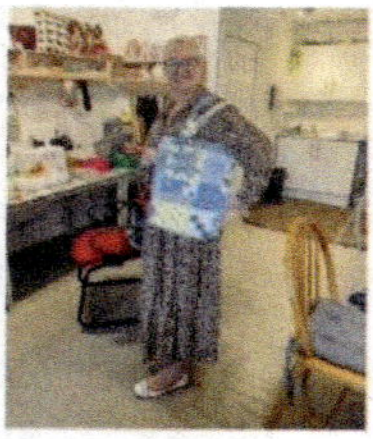
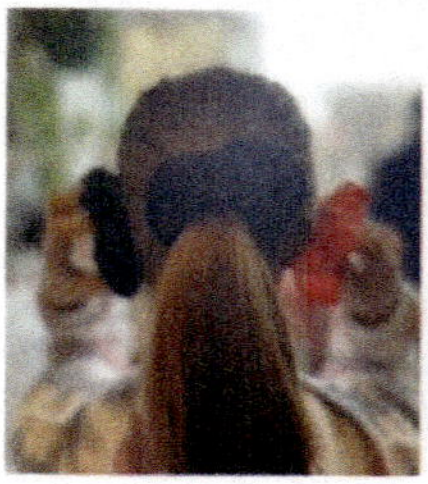
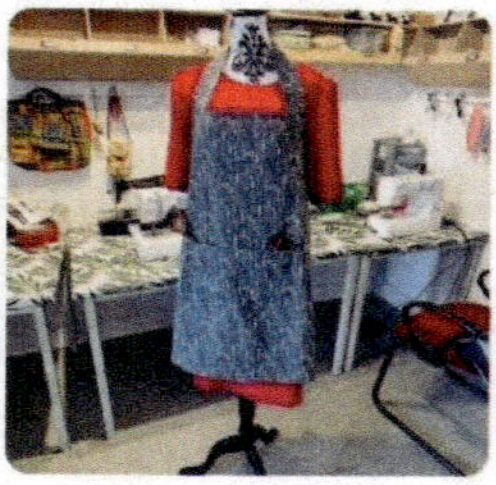
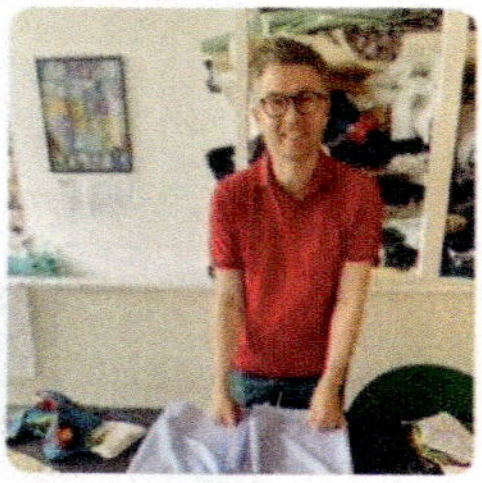
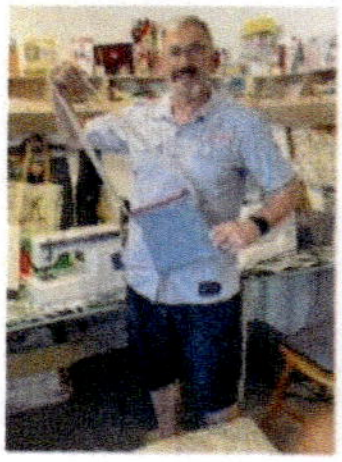
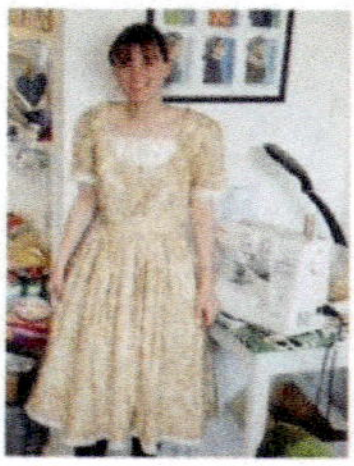
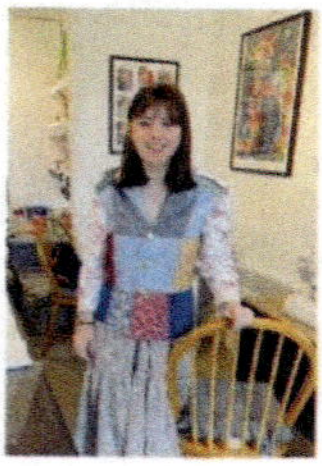

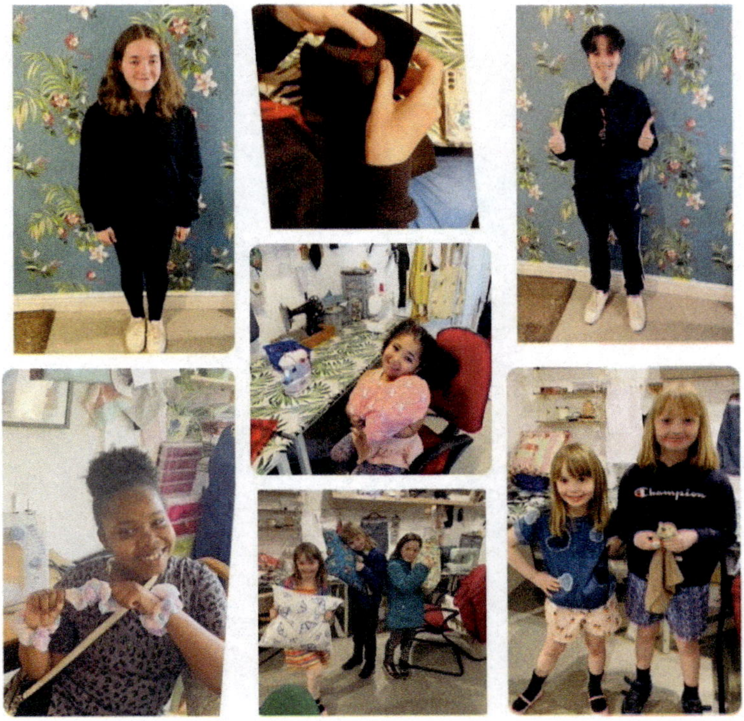
Champion

Lastly, I encourage you to share the gift of sewing with others. Teach a friend, mentor a child, or help a fellow enthusiast who may be struggling. By doing so, you're not just sharing a craft; you're passing on a sense of empowerment, creativity, and well-being.

As you continue your sewing and well-being journey, remember that it's a path without a final destination. It's a voyage of growth, self-discovery, and joy that extends far beyond the seams of your creations.

May your journey be filled with inspiration, community, and the ever-present reminder that each stitch holds the promise of creativity, fulfillment, and a life well-lived.

The author of this book is a dedicated and experienced professional who brings a unique blend of expertise from the fields of healthcare and the art of sewing. With nearly four decades of nursing and midwifery experience, the author's journey has been one of compassion, care, and a deep understanding of the human condition.

Nurtured in a small Yorkshire town known as Huddersfield, the author has extended this nurturing spirit into their own sewing school. In this cozy and welcoming studio, individuals from various walks of life and age groups, spanning from 6 years to 88 years, find a place where they can learn the art of sewing.

The sewing school isn't just a place of craft; it's a thriving community where people come together to explore their creative potential. It's a reflection of the author's belief in the power of sewing to enrich lives, foster connections, and inspire personal growth.

This book is a glimpse into the author's passion for sharing the art of sewing with a wider audience. The knowledge and insights garnered through years of healthcare practice have been thoughtfully integrated into the content of this book, providing a holistic perspective on how sewing can enhance mental and emotional well-being.

It is a heartfelt invitation to join the author on a journey through the transformative world of sewing, and a reflection of the author's sincere desire to empower others to embrace the craft and discover the boundless potential it offers for personal growth and well-being.

Printed in Great Britain
by Amazon